Robert McMurdy

Sketch of Joseph Benson Foraker

Robert McMurdy

Sketch of Joseph Benson Foraker

ISBN/EAN: 9783337425715

Printed in Europe, USA, Canada, Australia, Japan

Cover: Foto ©Thomas Meinert / pixelio.de

More available books at **www.hansebooks.com**

JOSEPH BENSON FORAKER.

It is said with reference to the duty of citizens at the polls, " Principles and not men ;" and, again, that only the character of candidates for office is to be considered. Is not the true maxim, " Men, and also principles?"

We have in Judge Foraker, both the noble, pure and patriotic man, and sound and well-tried principles. Nothing from his birth has been suggested that needs defense or apology. Hon. B. Butterworth says of him:

" He is a man without a flaw in intellect or morals. I would trust him with my dearest interests. If I lay on my death-bed and J. B. Foraker took my hand and said, ' I will look after your little ones,' I should be entirely satisfied. I know him to be afraid of but one thing—to do wrong."

Foraker's opponent, Judge Hoadley, admits the very temperate and pure mode of life of the Republican candidate for Governor. He says " J. B. Foraker ain't the man who would ever say a thing which he was conscious was untrue," even in politics.

Judge Foraker, at fourteen years of age, while on the farm, became a communicant of the church, and so continues. His piety is not ostentatious, but quiet and modest. He courts not business nor promotion by his religious association, nor by any connection with any society whatever.

FORAKER'S NOMINATION.

Judge Foraker's nomination was not of the ordinary political sort. It was without the usual political conferences. It was without effort upon his part. He did not seek it. He did not even desire it. The *Enquirer* said of Foraker, "He is not an office-seeker." The candidacy for Governor came to him from the people, from his neighbors, from his clients, from the private soldiers. It was free, hearty, enthusiastic, whole-souled. When it was generally determined that the candidate for Governor must be sought in southern Ohio, men of cool reflection and judgment, men of business and of morals, men of patriotic record, and men of patriotic impulse at various points, turned with spontaniety to Judge Foraker.

When the gubernatorial candidacy was seriously pressed upon Foraker, he thought of the regular duties of his office, of his fond wife and dear children, and of his domestic and social happiness, although all was plain and ordinary in his $3,000 house on the airy hills. Ever ready to serve his country, he thought the sacrifice great. He had made little more than a living in his honest practice, and in his honest administration of office. He could see before him only self-denial and continued scantiness of income. He coveted not mere honor. In his full heart he said to his friends :

" If Mr. ——— will make the race, you can draw on me for $1,000 for the campaign fund, but I refuse to contribute the smallest amount for my own candidacy." But the people said, our candidate you must be.

They had known Judge Foraker in the humbler, and they could trust him in the higher sphere of duty. He came before the people of Ohio as did Lincoln of Illinois, and as did Grant in his army promotion. As Lincoln was not the choice of politicians, nor Grant that of the generals, so Foraker's meritorious properties were first appreciated and recognized by the people. He was the choice of the people of his section, and is that of the whole State for governor, and his character as developing in the canvas, is giving him a reputation among the people of the country at large.

Views of political preferment beyond the position of governor were presented to encourage consent. He frankly said that he had no ulterior ambition ; that he preferred home and his profession, and his regular income ; that he could give but two years to his State and party ; that if thought necessary, he consented to this arduous service as he would renewedly enter upon the defense of his country, against domestic or foreign foe.

There was a general feeling over the State for a new man. The people wanted purity of character, and freedom for political combination.

After consent was given to be a candidate, he said, " I shall do nothing to create a boom for myself at the convention. I shall set no wires. The convention must settle the question."

The prayer at the opening of the convention was answered, that the " men nominated should be men of integrity and honor, of purity and of blameless life ; men who will do justly, who love mercy, and walk humbly before God."

Hon. Mr. Watson said in convention:

" More than twenty years ago, when Republicanism was the only power that was guiding this nation in the darkness of the civil war, a boy sixteen years of age entered the army as a private soldier. He sought neither fame nor glory. His only love was love for his country. His highest and holiest ambition was to fight in the ranks and for the flag. A year later, for special bravery on the battle-field, he was made a captain—the youngest captain in all that mighty host that battled for the stars. He was with that magnificent army—the grandest that ever stepped to martial music—whose achievements thrilled the nation with joy and the world with wonder as it marched to the sea and restored the flag to eternal supremacy in the land of its banishment."

His nomination was made by acclamation, followed by a scene of wild enthusiasm. Delegates rose in their places, and jumping on their chairs waved their hats and handkerchiefs frantically. The spirit of the movement animated all. Shout after shout, hurrah after hurrah went up, and the noise was beyond description. Even the sedate assembly of gentlemen on the stage forgot their dignity and reserve and joined in the tumultuous applause. The great sound was heard in the street, and thus the fact of Foraker's nomination was known to the outside world.

Among the good things in the Judge's speech of acceptance before the convention is this:

" The twenty-five years of Republican rule have been twenty-five years of triumph—triumph in war, triumph in peace, triumph at home, and triumph abroad, —until the whole globe has come to be circled with a living current of respect and esteem for the American flag and the American name that is absolutely without a parallel in the case of any other nation on the face of the earth." [Applause.]

The reporters at the convention said that Judge Foraker's speeches, extempore as they were, were exceptionally free from grammatical or constructional errors. There is no pretence of eloquence, but his speeches are ringing in well chosen, crisp language.

After the nomination prominent Democrats in southern Ohio testified   to the Judge's worth

Hon. Thos. Paxton declared him to be "an honor to the bar, an excellent citizen, a worthy gentleman."

Judge Wilson said: "Foraker is no fossil, and represents the progressive elements of his party. Judge Foraker's nomination is the very best that the Republican party could have made. He is a man of ability, of fine character, and as courteous a public officer as ever officiated. He deserves all the warm friends he has made in his official career."

Hon. Mr. Follett said, "Foraker is a strong and a good man."

Hon. Wm. Jordan considered Judge Foraker "a man of eminent ability, and socially very popular."

Representative Butterworth said, "No one doubts the character of Foraker. His record as a soldier, citizen, and lawyer is brilliant. Every part of his record from the cradle has been searched, and there is not a flaw in it. A party, that has had in its heart to nominate such a man, who represents such a pure and exalted morality, deserves to be victorious."

Hon. Mr. Townsend said at Athens that "Foraker is a high-minded citizen, with qualifications of the highest order—patriotism, sincerity, and honesty. His appearance wins. He is prudent, thoughtful, and a man who does not blunder. In his speeches he is judicial, with depth and dignity. Foraker can not be the tool of any man. His dignity protects him from such insinuations. He is too great a man to be subordinate long anywhere."

Hon. Thos. M'Dougall said at Magnetic Springs of Judge Foraker:

"For many years my warm personal friend, my associate at the bar, and my neighbor, I can speak of him from personal knowledge. People say of him he has no record, What do they mean? True, he has not the record of a political acrobat. * * * * He did not seek, did not need to seek, his nomination. There are no heart-burnings, no factional fights attached to his record. * * * * Ben. Foraker has nothing to explain, no apologies to make, no telegrams to send. * * * * Ben. Foraker—his only record is that of a loyal and affectionate son, a brave and brilliant soldier, an honorable, able, and conscientious judge, an honest, manly, and patriotic citizen, and a loving and devoted husband and father.

"'And thus he bears without abuse
The grand old name of gentleman.'

"Eminently qualified and completely equipped, the office sought him by acclamation, with honor and credit, and he has more than fulfilled in his conduct of the campaign, the high expectations of those of us who knew him best and had formed of him.

"'From men like these Ohio's greatness springs
That makes her loved at home, revered abroad;
Princes and lords are but the breath of kings—
An honest man is the noblest work of God.'

"In him you have one whose heart is true to law, to liberty, to right, who has the brain to plan and the courage to execute the purposes of such a heart. When, some years ago, the convention of which I was a member nominated him, then comparatively unknown in our city, for Judge of the Superior Court of our city, people said he had no record, and asked. 'Who is he?' They soon found out who he was. I knew him then; I know him now. When nominated for governor the same cry arose, 'He has no record.' 'Who is he?' They are finding out who he is."

Senator Sherman in his address at Cincinnati said that he never saw Judge Foraker till he met him at the state convention, and he was immediately pleased with his bearing, with his manner, his speech, and his conduct; he was gentle, kind, intelligent; but firm and strong. The conversation he had with him before his nomination impressed upon him that he was a man worthy to carry the Republican banner; he has made no mistake in his canvass, but has borne the Republican banner on from victory to victory.

WHAT THE TIMES DEMAND.

" God give us men a time like this demands,
   Great hearts, strong minds, true faith, and willing hands;
   Men whom the just of office does not kill,
   Men whom the spoils of office can not not buy,
   Men who possess an opinion and a will,
   Men who have honor, who will not lie."

FORAKER'S BIRTH AND EARLY HOME.

Like Lincoln and Grant, our candidate for governor was born July 5, 1846, among the hills and in the country, and like Lincoln and Harrison, in a log cabin ; born the second son and fifth child, one mile north of Rainsboro, and ten miles due-east of Hillsboro, Highland County, Ohio, on the Chillicothe and Milford turnpike. The Judge's father frequently has said that Saturday, the fourth, there was a militia muster at Rainsboro, in connection with the anniversary, and that on account of the Mexican war which commenced that year, and was then in progress, there was an unusual excitement about it, and he was especially anxious to attend. On account of the Judge's expected arrival, he stayed at home and cradled wheat all day.

The Judge is one of eleven children, six boys and five girls ; two of whom, one boy and one girl, died in infancy. The remaining nine, grown to manhood, are still living, except Burch, his oldest brother, who won position, honor, and respect, and died at the age of thirty-four.

His sisters living, are Sarah Elizabeth, wife of Milton McKeehan; Louisa Jane, widow of Samuel Amen; Maggie Reece, wife of Wm. C. Newell, son of the old miller, and all resident at Hillsboro. His brothers are James Ross, a law partner of the Judge, and Charles Elliott, and Creighton, at home.

In the wild and picturesque valley of Rocky Fork, in Highland County, Ohio, was Foraker's paternal home for ten years, in the log cabin near Rainsboro, and nine miles from Greenfield.

Scenery, hills, the country, climate, and honest and sturdy neighbors had somewhat to do with puerile development; but parental character and care vastly more.

Into the Rocky Fork Valley of Paint Creek, David Reese came in 1802, from Virginia, on account of his detestation of slavery, and as a pioneer in what was then a wilderness. He cleared his farm and had not completed his task when, in 1812, he entered the army and served on the northern frontier. He represented Highland County in the State legislature—an honest and respected citizen. One of his daughters, the Judge's mother, married Henry S. Foraker, the father of the Judge, whose family had also settled in Highland County, moving from Delaware because of their distaste of slavery. Into their possession came the old farm and saw and grist-mill, where Joseph Benson spent most of his early days.

SAW-MILL AND SCHOOL.

In this old saw-mill was often the church-gathering on Sunday for the pioneer families, the preacher putting his Bible and hymn book on the top of an up-ended puncheon, and the congregation seated on improvised benches. This was the early church of the Foraker's and Rees'.

THE OLD SCHOOL HOUSE.

The school-house was a poor cabin, deserted by its original tenant for a better location. The ventilation was abundant, and the scholars picked out the clay of the chinking until every cranny was open to the wind. The teachers could sit near the fire-place, the pupils write with their faces toward the window, but in conning their lessons straddling the benches without a back, the girls on one side and the boys on the other of the room.

THE OLD MILL. (See page 13.)

THE FORAKER LOG CABIN.

The reign of the rod was not disputed by the teacher, who taught but few branches in winter, and wrought in summer. The tramp of the pupils for miles through the untrodden snow, with the cold dinner, was of itself discipline enough.

Such was the pioneer school of the Foraker's, at Rocky Fork.

A correspondent of the *Commercial Gazette* in a late visit to Highland gives us, information as to Foraker's parents. Upon his inquiry as to Ben's father, the store-keeper of the hamlet at Rainsboro, replied :

" Well, he's in the back of the store now, trading some butter."

Looking in the direction indicated, an elderly man, dressed as a farmer, with sunburn face and hands, was seen. His broad-brimmed straw hat, which was darkened and formless from long exposure to all kinds of weather, was pushed back from his forehead, and his thin, snowy locks were in full view. He is, every inch of him, a hale, hearty old man, whose appearance tells of a head stored with good, sound common sense, and he belongs to that class whom one delights to refer to as the 'bone and sinew.' His distinguished son resembles him very much, the father's high brow, and nose with the firm, open nostrils, being duplicated in the son. He had just come in from the farm, bringing with him six great rolls of yellow, sweet-smelling butter, which Mrs. Foraker had churned but a few hours before, and which he was exchanging for groceries.

"What do you want it in ?" the store-keeper was heard to ask.

"My wife told me to get it in sugar, to put up her blackberries and things."

While the sugar was being put up, the correspondent introduced himself to Mr. Foraker, who straightway insisted that he should accompany him home, and, as it was near dinner time, an extra plate would be put upon the table.

"There's always enough, and it's good, hearty country fare," he urged; "but I'm sorry you came all the way from Cincinnati, and I didn't know beforehand, for we can't make an extra spread for you now. You see, one of our neighbors is threshing, and we lent our hired girl to help them, and so Mrs. Foraker is all alone ; but our friends are always welcome."

THE FORAKER FARM.

The Foraker farm, which consists of 170 acres of good upland, is on the Hillsboro pike, from which the plain, comfortable house, painted white, with reddish-brown shutters, is plainly visible. The immense barn is between the house and the road, and the first thing one sees on reaching the place is a towering heap of wheat straw, which has just been threshed, and which is piled so high as to fairly eclipse the barn. In front of the house are aged trees, in whose grateful shade unnumbered chickens and curious young turkeys lazily take their noon-time rest, scarcely moving as the newspaper visitor makes his way up the walk. On the porch are Mr. Foraker and his son, Charles, a younger brother of the Judge's, who is determined to be a farmer, who greet the traveler hospitably, and all these engage in a political discussion, while the lady of the house can be heard bustling about inside getting dinner.

THE ARMY.

"Mr. Foraker," asked your correspondent, "didn't you object to the Judge entering the army?"

"I did, but the boy was set upon it, so I let him go. You see his elder brother, Burch, was in a law office in Hillsboro, and when he enlisted, Ben thought he must go and fill his place. By and by he caught the fever, too, and said he was going to be a soldier. I told him that he was not mature enough; that he could not endure the long marches with the heavy burdens he would be obliged to carry; that he would become sick, go to the hospital and perhaps die. I thought it was good sensible advice to tell a boy of seventeen that he could not do a man's work. But my refusal weighed upon his mind and so I had to let him go. In his first letter home, from Virginia, I think it was, he jubilantly wrote that while he was carrying a load for a pony and was feeling well as ever, men of two hundred pounds were dropping by the road side."

"Did you think that the Judge was going to be nominated?"

"I felt it in my bones, and when the day arrived I didn't need any telegram to tell me what had happened. Before the Convention I received a letter from Ben saying that if he was nominated, Hoadley would be worthy any man's steel, and that it would be no disgrace to be beaten by such a man, while to be victorious would be honor indeed."

"Were you at the Convention?"

"No, it was right in the middle of harvesting, and I could not be spared."

FATHER AND SON.

"I suppose you are proud of your boy?"

"Proud of him? proud of Ben? Why, I'm his father, and I'm prouder of him since the campaign opened than ever. I knew that Ben was pretty solid, but whether he could compete with Hoadley on the stump was a matter of doubt. Now, of course, I'm partial, for I'm his father, but when it comes to facts I know that Ben's always on hand."

"Have you seen him since he was nominated?"

"He wrote me just after the Convention that he wanted to come here and rest for a day or two, and then he wrote again that he was kept so busy that he din't know if he would ever come, but I saw him when he made his Fourth of July speech at Leesburg. For a long time I tried to get him alone, and finally we succeeded in slipping out into the bushes, and I stole a half hour's chat with him."

"And what did you talk about?"

"I told him that I had read every word of his speeches, and that so far he had made no mistakes, and to be very careful. I told him to keep out of anything low or mean, to be conscientious, but he don't need any such advice from me. He's got more sense as regards politics and behaving himself than I ever will have, but he listens like a good son to everything I say."

"Tell me, Mr. Foraker, are you going to take an active part in the campaign?"

"All his old friends in Highland County are going to vote for him without being asked, but I am a judge of election, and feel that to be perfectly square I should be above electioneering."

"How did the Judge happen to choose the law?"

"I guess it was natural in him. When he was getting his education I was asked what I was going to make of him. I always had an ambition to educate my children. I always felt the need of a good education myself, and I prepared my boys so that when the time came they could themselves decide upon what they wanted to do. Ben first wanted to be a soldier, but after a bit he decided to be a lawyer. When he went to Cincinnati I told him that he couldn't live there, that it was full of lawyers and that he would starve, but he said 'if you want to do business you must go where it is done,' and so he went. He only knew one man there when he went, but he got along all the same."

MOTHER AND SON.

And then the proud old father told the story of his "boy's" triumphs and successes, of his goodness and kindness, and his eyes lighted with pleasure as he spoke. While he was still chatting Mrs. Foraker came to the door and announced that dinner was ready. She is an active old lady, a typical farmer's wife, with sharp, kindly twinkling eyes, and hands that are ever busy, and in seeing her, one understands from whence comes the Judge's indomitable courage and unceasing work. And oh how proud she is of her son ! Her face fairly beams with joy at the mere mention of his name, and when his brilliant career is spoken of she smiles in an excess of happiness. She said that she had been "putting up" blackberries all morning and that the visitor would have to excuse the ordinary farmer's fare, and looked dubious when your correspondent told her that an honest home meal was fit for a king. And now that the dinner is a thing of the past he can bear witness that Mrs. Foraker is as excellent a cook as her son is a political speaker. Of course the conversation at the table was almost entirely concerning "Ben."

THE COFFEE-SACK BREECHES.

"Mrs. Foraker," said the writer, "nearly everybody in Ohio wants to know the truth about those coffee-sack breeches. Now tell me, did you ever make him such a pair, or is it only a campaign fabrication ?"

"Oh, no," the lady replied with a laugh, "it is the solemn truth, and what is more he wore them out. You see it was in the fall when Ben was about ten years old, and the men folks were all busy building a dam, and in the house the girl and myself had all we could do preparing for them, as there were a lot of extra hands. Ben wsa under the necessity to have another pair of pants or he couldn't go to school. Everybody was too busy to go to town to buy any cloth, and for a time I didn't know what to do. All at once I thought of an inside coffee sack that was in the house, and so I made the breeches out of it. When I showed them to the boy, he look disappointed and said : 'I don't want to wear them, the boys will make fun of me.' 'Never mind,' said I, 'if you make a smart man people will never ask what kind of pants you wore when a boy."

"Yes," broke in Mr. Foraker, "that's the truth of it, and it wasn't from extreme poverty as some of the papers said. My wife is a saving kind of woman—a fortune to any man—and that coffee sack just happened to be handy." [Foraker's coffee-sack breeches are not yet worn out. They will stick to him like Grant's hides, Old Abe's axe, and Washington's little hatchet. Such a man will win in Ohio and the country all the time.]

"There never was a better boy to his mother than Ben," continued Mrs. Foraker, "and he helped round the house as good as any girl. I taught all my boys to wash, iron, milk, cook, spin, and Ben used to have to pick the geese."

THE CORN.

"Ben," supplemented the father, "was one of the kind of boys that thought that if any of the rest of his companions was able to do anything he could do it too. One day his elder brother, Burch, put up thirty-three shocks of corn, for which I paid him one dollar, and Ben felt that he ought to earn some money as well. I told him that he was too small to do such hard work, for the corn was strong and high, but he said he was going to try. That day I went to the fair, and when I came back I found that he had put up his thirty-three shocks. He was not tall enough to tie them, and so he had got his little sister to stand on a chair and do it, while he held the stalks in place. It was a powerful day's work for a boy, and I don't see how he ever did it."

Running about one of the pastures on the farm is an old, dun-colored pony, which was owned as a colt and broken in by the now Judge. There is a story told that when he was still a "beardless youth," he fell in love with a Mt. Carmel girl, and so as to be near her he refused to go to the Rainsboro Sunday-school, but rode his pony to the one which was attended by the object of his affection. But, alas! for the poor boy. When he went off to fight his country's battles, she forgot him and married another fellow. The pony was ridden after Morgan, at the time of his celebrated Ohio raid, by Mr. Foraker, and at present the little son of the Judge, when he is visiting at the farm, rides the ancient nag to the Post-office for the semi-weekly mail, and, by-the-way, the farm was bought and presented to his parents by their ever-thoughtful son.

THE SECRET.

In the foregoing, we have the secret largely of Judge Foraker's character and success. It should be added that these parents are pious Methodists, with their morning and evening worship, with their regard for the sacredness of Sunday and of religious institutions, with their temperate habits and honest ways, and with their observance of the maxim not to "make haste to be rich." They had moved from a state cursed with slavery to begin life on free soil. They read little, but read thoroughly. They study the Bible and good books. They are most familiar with the Methodist commentary on the Bible—that of Joseph Benson. Hence the Judge was baptized Joseph Benson. Josephus' and Bunyan's Pilgrim's Progress are family text-books.

GUBERNATORIAL PREDICTION.

The boy, Foraker, was noted from earliest years for energy, perseverance, truth, and honesty. He was a hard-wrought boy, ploughing with a span of horses when ten years old. He took no pleasure in depressing his companions; and while frequently aid-ing them in tasks and lessons, he excelled by his own innate strength. He led naturally. He was the chosen chief for victory in sports and games. In one of his feats of daring this barefooted and berry-stained boy, with pockets bulging with green apples, fell into the mill-race, and was rescued by Samuel Newell, for a long time miller on Rocky Fork, who so admired his wise pluck in struggling for life that that the rescuer said that boy would be governor some day, and, who, again, a few years after, when he had a discussion with a Democratic relative, picked up his favorite boy and said, "We'll beat you some day for governor with this farmer boy."

THE SPARGURS AT RAINSBORO.

September 15, 1883, the Spargurs of Ohio gathered on the farm of Jno. Bedkey, in view of the site of the Foraker log cabin. "Uncle Joe" Spargur was chairman. Rev. Cunningham, of Hillsboro, offered prayer. Rev. Somner, of Virginia, gave a Bible talk. Mrs. Bedkey's Spargur re-union song was sung, to an air, the product of the music-loving Milton W. Spargur. After dinner Hon. H. L. Dickey's speech was on "Character"—its importance illustrated in the families of Rainsboro before him. Mr. A. D. Wiggins followed. Judge Foraker was then introduced, by "Uncle Joe" Spargur, as *Ben Foraker Spargur*, when the assembled six thousand made the forests ring with shouts of recognition and of their fondness for their neighbor, their soldier boy. No introduction was necessary, as the Judge was at his boyhood home, and among the friends and companions of his youthful days, where he had romped, and among the "boys in blue," with whom in riper years, but a boy still, he marched to meet unblushing treason in battle array.

THE BREECHES AT HILLSBORO.

September 19 is said to have been the greatest day in the history of Highland. From far and near came Highland's hosts to pay tribute to her honored son. The streets were crowded, and it was almost impossible to get around. A moderate limit places the number at six thousand, which has only been exceeded once before—during the Brough-Vallandigham campaign. Judge Foraker arrived on the noon train from South Salem, where he addressed a great audience, September 18, in the campus of the academy. Here the Judge attended school after the war, and was personally known. The boys greeted him as Ben, both Republicans and Democrats, and Ben recalled the names of Beech and Amos and hundreds of his old school and army friends. At Hillsboro the Currier Band of Cincinnati escorted the Judge to the Kramer House. Here he was waited upon by the entire conference of the African Methodist Church, with their bishop. Visitors were introduced by Col. Glen of the 89th, his old commander. From Paint Township (the Judge's) came a long procession, headed by a dun pony, which the Judge rode when a boy, and followed by wagons containing thirty-eight boys with coffee-sack breeches, and a number of girls, dressed in red, white, and blue. One of the wagons bore the motto, "Paint Township will Whitewash Hoadly." Flags were shown on all the principal buildings, and across Main Street hung an immense banner bearing the words, "Old Highland welcomes her honored son, Ben Foraker, the next Governor of Ohio." Banners bore numerous mottoes, among them, " This boy will be our Governor yet'— Samuel Newell;" "Paint Township will whitewash Hoadly;" on the wagon bearing the boys in coffee-sack breeches, "We will be voters by and by."

J. B. FORAKER, Co. A, 89th Regt., O. V. I.

Born on the day succeeding the Fourth of July, Ben was an extraordinarily patriotic lad. This miller farmer boy of Rocky Fork enlisted as a private, July 14, 1862, in Company A, of the

89th Ohio Infantry, the first man mustered into his regiment, and the last man mustered out.

His chief and perhaps his only act of positive disobedience and wilful resistance against parental authority was when he made a bundle of his scanty wardrobe and started off for the recruiting rendezvous, depositing his baggage in a corner of the car of a freight-train, determined to go to the defense of his country as a religious duty. When his departure was discovered, it was agreed to leave the matter to his brother, Burch, and he decided that the boy should go, as he thought he had a mission of patriotism.

Captain Glenn (afterward colonel) in raising his company, at Hillsboro, promised the position of first or orderly sergeant to the soldier securing the greatest number of recruits; and that of second sergeant to the private bringing in the next largest number. Ben went rapidly over Clermont, Ross, and Highland counties, and was soon in possession of the promised place. A boy of but sixteen years of age, he said that he knew nothing of military affairs and generously and gracefully yielded the place to the private next to him in efficient recruiting, he taking the second sergeantcy, August 26th, 1862. This was in the second year of the war, Ben being only fifteen at the breaking out of the rebellion. His brother, the lamented Captain Burch Foraker, had preceded him in the service of his country. Reluctantly did his fond parents consent to part with another son.

The 89th, without having been in military retreat and discipline, was hastened into a service at once active and severe. Ben was in its exhausting marches, its camp privations, and its losses by battle and disease. He was made second lieutenant January 24th, 1863; and then, first lieutenant, February 1st, 1864. Late in the summer of 1863 he was sent to Ohio to recruit for the regiment. He was on this duty when the famous battle of Chickamauga took place—that battle of which the author of "Ohio in the War" said:

"Falling back on Chattanooga, our army went into intrenchments. Monday morning at nine o'clock, Surgeon Crew, the only commissioned officer in the fight left, all being killed, wounded, or taken prisoners, of the Eighty-ninth, sick with jaundice, and just able to ride on horseback, found himself half a mile in front of our line of battle with forty wounded, twenty sick and seventy-five well men,—all that was left of the Eighty-ninth."

" Captain Jolly, who had been at home recruiting, arrived at Chatta-nooga the day after the battle, with the sick who had recovered. He was promoted to Major, and took command. The Eighty-ninth soon mustered two hundred men. For six weeks it lay in the marble quarry at Chatta-nooga with shell bursting over its camp from Lookout Mountain, subsist-ing on half rations, scantily clothed, and braving the rigors of winter. It witnessed Hooker's charge up the steeps of Lookout Mountain, and joined in the shout of victory as the enemy gave way and fled. The next day, when the charge was made on Mission Ridge, Major Jolly, at the head of his little band of two hundred men, led them to victory in the front of the attacking column."

Foraker, then but seventeen years old, reached Chattanooga the night before the charge of Mission Ridge. Receiving no orders, he entered his regiment as it was going into battle, instantly took command of his company, led it to the charge, and was chival-rously the first man of his regiment over the enemy's works. He served in the field with the Third Division of the Fourteenth Ar-my Corps, Army of the Cumberland. He was with the Eighty-ninth at Dalton, Georgia; in Rocky Face charge, February 25th; in the campaign against Atlanta, and in the battles of Buzzard's Roost, Resaca, Burnt Hickory, Peach Tree Creek, Hoover's Gap, Lookout Mountain, Mission Ridge, Ringold, Kenesaw Mountain, Eutoy Creek, Averysboro, and Bentonville.

After the fall of Atlanta he was placed on duty with the Signal Corps. In Sherman's March to the Sea, November, 1864, he was on the Staff of Major General Slocum, commanding the army of Georgia. He remained with Slocum in the campaigns to the Sea and through the Carolinas. He was mustered out June 13, 1865, while serving as Aid-de-Camp on Slocum's staff.

The U. S. Fleet lay off the mouth of the Savannah river, eight-een miles below the city, without knowledge that Sherman had reached Savannah. The river was as full of torpedos as the banks were of rebels. Foraker was selected to let the loyal people of the country know through the fleet that Sherman had finished his campaign. Foraker secured a row-boat and the services of two faithful negroes as rowers, and in the night, with one orderly, be-gan his perilous adventure. The boat ran aground several times in the darkness and barely escaped capsizing, took to the fleet the first news of Savannah's capture, as he will in October, send the message all over our patriotic country, that another battle for freedom has been fought and won.

There are thousands of citizens of Ohio who can recall with great distinctness the days and weeks of agonizing suspense during Sherman's march from Atlanta to the sea, in November and December, 1864. How the great heart of the North fairly stood still, in anxiety to hear reliable tidings of his progress, and the condition of his army! What battles had been fought; what brave soldiers were slain or wounded? These were questions that were in every mind. No news came except through rebel sources, and there were stories of disaster to our army, put forth, as we afterwards knew to fire the flagging zeal of the Southern people, but they served to increase the anxiety of Ohio people who had thousands of husbands, sons and brothers in that army.

FORT M'ALLISTER

Was taken by assault, but Savannah still held out and offered a strong obstacle to our march. Finally, however, that city was taken, but there was no means of direct communication with the North to transmit the news, Foraker reached the fleet, carrying Sherman's famous dispatch to the President, which our readers read on the morning of December 26, 1864, and which electrified the nation, as follows:

SAVANNAH, GA., July 22.

To His Excellency President Lincoln:

I beg to present to you as a Christmas gift the city of Savannah, with one hundred and fifty heavy guns and a plenty of ammunition, and also about twenty-five thousand bales of cotton.

W. T. SHERMAN, Major General.

The safe conduct of that dispatch was a daring feat, requiring the highest degree of courage and judgment. People will readily remember the incident and the dispatch, but the modest young bearer of it has been known to but few persons until late years, though he is to be better known in the future.

His superior officer in Military Division, Mississippi, said in his report: "* * * Lieut H. W. Howgate and J. B. Foraker succeeded in getting a part of the rebels' signal corps.

Captain James M. McClintock, with his detachment with the right wing, acting in accordance with general instructions given by me to all the signal officers of the army of Georgia, to use every possible effort to communicate with the fleet on our coming near the coast, on the 12th inst. he took with him Lieut. Sampson and several men, and, went to Dr. Cheeve's rice mill, on the Great Ogeechee, within three miles of Fort McAllister to try, if possible, to communicate with the fleet if any portion of it came up the river. During the night they tried to draw the fire of the Fort if possible, and during the night threw up rockets to attract the attention of any vessel that might chance to be in hearing or in sight, but without success. During the day and night a section of artillery (twenty pound parrots) under command of Capt. Degrasse came down and fired at the Fort. During the day and during the night of the 12th instant, until midnight, a gun was fired every ten minutes, and at the same time a rocket was sent up by the officers, but without any success.

On the 13th instant communication was opened with Lieuts. Sherfey and Adams, who accompanied the Second Division Fifteenth Army Corps, under orders to take the Fort. General Sherman, who was at the Rice Mill Station, sent his orders by signal to Gen. Hazen, to make the assault on the Fort.

IN SIGHT.

At 3 P. M. a vessel came up the river in sight. They now called the vessel, and after some time a signal flag was hoisted. I ordered them to put themselves in communication with the officer on board ; but instead of answering the call, he began to call them ; they answered his call, and at once opened communication with the fleet. The officer on board the vessel asked " Who is there?" In reply, General Sherman sent the following message, "General Sherman's Army is now here all well. Savannah and Fort McAllister closely invested." A number of messages passed over the line, when at 5 P. M., Fort McAllister was carried by assault.

General Sherman now sent the following message to the vessel :

" Fort McAllister just taken by assault; come to the fort immediately." Communication was opened from the station at the Rice Mill immediately after taking the Fort.

On he 14th inst., Lieuts. Dunlap and J. B. Kelley relieved Capt. J. McClintock and Lieut. Sampson, at the Rice Mill Station. On the 16th inst. I received orders from General Sherman to establish a line from Fort McAllister to his headquarters, some ten (10) miles distant. On this line Lieuts. Sherfey, Shellabarger, and Worley did duty. Some work was done on this line

On the 21st inst. the enemy evacuated the city, and I at once went into the city to superintend the opening of communication with Fort Pulaski, and also to communicate with the fleet, or Major General Foster. * * *

LIEUT. J. B. FORAKER

Was ordered to proceed down the river and open communication with Fort Pulaski, if any signal officer was there. But finding it impossible to go far enough, owing to the marshy nature of the ground, he returned to Fort Jackson, procured a small boat, and pressing two negroes for oarsmen, he, with his flagman (second class private Thomas E. Matteson), started for Fort Pulaski, some nine miles distant, which point he reached some time after dark. He communicated soon after with Maj. General Foster, in person, some two miles off. He was the first to give him the news of our troops occupying the city of Savannah. On the following day he returned with General Foster to the city. The line from Headquarters Military Division of Mississippi to Fort McAllister was broken up and one established from the latter place to Rose Dew Battery.

In conclusion, too much cannot be said of the conduct, efforts and energy displayed by the officers of the corps in trying to establish communication with the fleet. * * * Also Lieut. J. B. Foraker, acting signal officer, in carrying out his orders, in a small boat over unknown waters, almost at the peril of his life.

Of the other officers and men, to whom no fine opportunities were presented to distinguish themselves, all have willingly, faithfully, and well performed their duty. I am Colonel, very respectfully,

Your ob't serv't, SAM. BACHTELL,

Capt. and Sig. Officer, U. S. A.

Lieut. Col. WM. J. L. NICODEMUS, Act. Chief Sig. Officer, U. S. A.

I certify the above is a true copy of my official report of services performed by my command, for the month of December, 1864.

SAM. BACHTELL, Late Chief Sig. Officer, Mil. Div. Miss.,

and Brevet Lieut. Colonel."

The confidence reposed in this soldier-youth was manifested upon various occasions.

When Sherman had deflected his columns, and with confidence of no further interruption, sought to open communication with Schofield, Johnson, with his usual skill, had fortified his position of defense. When Sherman's left wing was marching with the belief of freedom from any attack, it came directly upon Johnson's skirmishers. The Union troops were driven in with some loss. Who was the trusted messenger sent by Slocum to Sherman to tell him that he (Slocum) was confronted by Johnson's whole army, and thus save the patriotic army and the campaign? Our Highland County soldier, who observed Slocum's injunction, "Be careful, but don't spare horse-flesh! He thus bearing the order for Hazen's division of the Fifteen Corps, and returning with it, reached the battle-field at three o'clock in the morning. It was by no political influence, or by the pleading of influential friends that Foraker was breveted captain, but for such services:

"Efficient services during the recent campaigns in Georgia and South Carolina, to date from March 19, 1865," as reads General Order No. 97, of the War Department.

The people of Ohio felt that patriotism needed a revival, and they turned to the honest, faithful, and patriotic soldier as their candidate, who enlisted at the age of sixteen, and had earned his position of honest respect when the country was almost in the agony of dissolution, and when men were falling in battle like leaves before the frost.

A well known private soldier writes :

" For sixteen years and more at all our soldiers' meetings and re-unions, we of the rank and file, while conceding to the officers a fair share of the civil offices, have kept demanding for the private soldiers some reasonable portion of the elective offices in our State and Nation.

To be candid, for myself I hardly ever expected to see the day when I would have the privilege of voting for a real live private for Governor of Ohio. But now, in obedience to this demand of at least one hundred thousand voters in Ohio, one of the rank and file of the Union Volunteer Army has at last been nominated for that great office. Foraker must serve the good purpose of showing those who sneer at us that a man may have been a private soldier and yet may be a great statesman besides.

Other titles Judge Foraker has of good right--judge, jurist, scholar, and all that—to recommend him to the respect and confidence of the people of Ohio; but his prominent recommendation among soldiers is the fact, and the fact it is, that he once wore the humble blouse and did the duty of a gallant private in the Union army. He was not one of those gilt-edged privates of whom we have so often read, who was only nominally for a day a private—with a full understanding that on the morrow the politicians would have a commission sent to him ; but he was at the front on the march, in battle, with his musket, knapsack and old canteen, just like the rest of the boys. He is our comrade by the strongest of ties. We must not let the politicians say to us hereafter, ' Here, now, you fellows have been asking us to nominate a private, and when we did so, you defeated Private Foraker.' Let every soldier in Ohio vote for Foraker."

The private soldiers of Ohio knew Foraker's soldier-worth and demanded and secured this private as candidate for governor of Ohio. As the officers in the person of Grant and of many others have been honored, so in Foraker is the whole rank and file of the army.

PATRIOTIC DETERMINATION.

Capt. James Duffy, the well-known Roman Catholic and Irish Democrat of Pickaway County, says that he will vote for Foraker. His language is:

"I think it my duty to God, my country, and myself. When we needed men to go to the front, Foraker, boy as he was, shouldered his musket and marched away. I was with him fighting for our country. He can be trusted in war and in peace. He risked his young life for us, while other candidates were feathering their own nest. As a soldier and a citizen, I shall vote for Foraker."

Captain Cable says, "While Foraker is a very popular candidate with the Ohio voters generally, he is especially so among the veterans, who are proud of their candidate and the boy soldier."

BEN FORAKER'S BREECHES—BY PRIVATE BILL JONES.

"Ben needed a new pair of pants when he was a boy, and Mrs. Foraker was too poor to buy the goods for them, and had nothing in the world to make them out of but an old coffee sack. Ben looked a little ashamed when he first put them on, but his mother said, "Never mind, my boy; if you grow up to be a good and useful man nobody will ever ask what kind of breeches you wore.'"—*Commercial Gazette's* Highland County Correspondence.

Old lady, you're just a leetle off
  In your britches pint of view—
The kind of britches a fellow wore
  Made a difference in sixty-two!

There was the chaps that wore them gray,
  With gray-backs in every hem,
And ragged and dirty—*but they was brave;*
  We shot, but *respected them.*

And there was them that sneaked at home
  And called us "Lincoln dogs"
And "hired cut-thr'ats" and all such stuff—
  Them fellers wore *butternut togs.*

I guess, old lady, about this time
  You've stumbled onto my cue,
And it is scarcely necessary to speak
  About the "boys in blue."

Yes, I was out in the Eighty-ninth,
  And fought the whole war through
With your boy Ben, and *I* can swear
  Ben Foraker's britches was blue.

For *I saw* him *go up Mission Ridge—*
  Ahead of the regiment, too,—
And jump *the works and straddle a gun,*
  So I had an excellent view

And we marched together to the sea
  And up through the Carolinas,
And Ben was with us *ev-e-ry time*
  Amongst the swamps and pines.

Just call on the boys of the Eighty-ninth
And ask them a question or two,
And you will find that your boy Ben
Was, *britches and heart, true blue!*

And when us fellers walk up to the polls
To vote for a Governor,
*We're agoing to ask "when we was out
What kind of britches he wore?"-*

A FEW EXTRACTS FROM FORAKER'S DIARY.

We have been privileged to inspect the diary of this patriotic young and private soldier. We have space for but a few extracts

June 5, 1863. . As tired a boy as you can ever find. .

June 6, 1863. . Very sick all day. Longed for home. Marched nine miles. After a rest, ordered to march again. Sicker than ever. . .

June 7. . Marched to Murfreesboro—twenty miles ; worse on the way and gave out. Rode to Col. Glenn's house—nine miles. . .

June 10. . Burch [his brother] came. Never so glad to see any one. . .

June 11. . Burch and myself went all over the battle-field. I saw enough to sicken my heart. War is a curse and our conflict a sad necessity. . .

June 16. Ten months to day since I left "Old Hillsboro." . . .

June 17. Night, and in charge of 155 men on the outpost—picketing. .

Lynchburg, Ohio, Oct. 8. 1863. Here trying to recruit for our regiment. Dull business. Hope I shall not be compelled to remain here long. The old 89th has been in the great battle of Chickamauga. I feel sadly disappointed in not being there. . . .

Oct. 13. . Much fun last night—burning "tar barrels" and hurrahing for Johnny Brough and the Union. . . . .

Oct. 14, Highland County has gone for the Union by a very decided majority. . . . . .

Oct. 15. An immense torch-light procession for the great Union victory in Highland County and Ohio. Brough's majority reported at seventy thousand. The supporters of Vallandingham look ashamed. . . .

Oct. 25. Low spirited—want to go to the regiment. . . . .

Nov. 10. Start for the regiment to-morrow. . . . .

Chattanooga, Dec. 4, 1863. Reached the regiment just in time to go into a fight. Don't like fighting well enough to make a profession of it. War is cruel, and when this conflict is over I shall retire from public life. . .

New Year's-day. Cold as Greenland, . Nothing to eat, scarcely any wood to burn, and enough work for ten men. . . .

Jan. 4. 1864. Would like to be in Hillsboro to-day to go to church. Many a poor soldier to-day hovers over his smoky fire, while the cold, heartless winds come tearing through his thin tent, almost freezing him to death, and yet you hear no word of complaint. They are the bravest men that ever composed an army ; and while my suffering is equal to their's, I feel proud of my condition—a clear conscience that I am doing my duty; and this affords me more comfort than all the enjoyments of home. I feel a pride rising in my bosom in realizing that I am a member of the old 14th Corps of the Army of the Cumberland. . . . . .

Feb. 5, 1864. . . Getting along well ; but would get along better if I were not on duty almost every day ; but what matters this ? I am serving my country, and this is consolation enough. . .

March 14. 1864. Would like to be at home, going to school and preparing myself for future duty; but my country calls and I remain. . .

From some memoranda of burials of soldiers the writer judges that our soldier lad read the burial service occasionally over a dead comrade, beginning, "Man that is born of a woman," etc.

TWO OF THE BOYS.

Mr. Doughty, of Company F, Eighty-ninth O. V. I.   (Foraker's old regiment), an invalid at the Soldiers' Home, said to a correspondent of the *Commercial-Gazette*, " That he knew Judge Foraker from the time of his enlistment to the close of the war. My company was next to his in the ranks and in camp, and I had opportunities for close acquaintance."
" How was he regarded by the boys ?"
"Nobody was more popular. He was so generous and unassuming that he was universally liked. When he was promoted he put on no airs. Neither did our Colonel Glenn, of Chillicothe. Yet it was unusual for men promoted from the ranks to behave so. 'Ben,' as we always called him, engaged in our sports, and was as much of a boy with us as ever, though he could be dignified when it was necessary and proper. I verily believe that there is not a man of the old Eighty-ninth but will vote for Foraker, no matter what may be his party."
"You look young. What was your age when you enlisted ?"
" I was only nineteen, just three years the senior of Judge Foraker, and had a fellow-feeling with him as a young man."
" Have you long been an invalid ?"
" Yes, my health early failed in the Kanawha Valley, where many were taken down with camp-fever. Since then I have scarcely been well."
" Does your regiment have re-unions ?"
" Yes, it is to have one at Amelia, on the Cincinnati Eastern, the twentieth of this month. Judge Foraker will be there, I have no doubt, and I intend going if I possibly can. It is a great honor to the Eighty-ninth to have a nominee for Governor, and the boys will show their appreciation, by helping their old comrade all they can."

Your correspondent then found another comrade of Foraker—Al. Bieber, of Company H, Forty-ninth O. V. I. Bieber is employed at Ritty's restaurant, (Dayton), and was glad to express his opinion of "Ben." He said that Ben never lost his popularity on account of promotion or anything else. " He was the same in manners from first to last," said Bieber. "A good many of those fellows when they got shoulder-straps on, wouldn't associate with the poor devils who hadn't the intelligence, or the influence, or the opportunity to get promoted. We couldn't all be officers, and Ben seemed to understand that, and think just as much of us anyhow."
" What's your politics?"
" I am a Republican, but if I were a Democrat, I would vote for Ben. He's my man, and I don't see why he isn't going to be elected, It looks to me as though nothing could stop him now. He has the start of the other man, and will be likely to keep it. It's just like him. When he was Orderly Sergeant he always had his reports and other papers ready before any one else."

THE TRUE SON AND A TRUE SOLDIER.

Extracts from correspondence of the young private with his parents.
In his letter from West Point, Va. Oct. 16, 1862., after describ-

ing the country and the situation of the army, he expresses his affection for "Company I," of his regiment, he being on detached service. He refers to the sad necessity of using churches at times for army quarters.

1862.

August 17, 1862. Camp Dennison: "* * We visited the hospitals. We saw hard sights, some with their arms cut to pieces, some with their legs shattered by balls and mangled. * * There are 100 secession prisoners here captured at Pittsburg. They all confess a determination not to join the army of the Confederacy again. * * Instead of the ring of the church bell, I hear the drums and the fife. * * Sunday is not known here."

September 20, 1862. Camp Shaler, Ky.: * * "I spent no money foolishly. * * We had Friday a nice flag presented by George Coleman, of Cincinnati.

Above Clifton, Va., Nov. 3, 1862. Father Dear. * * Two weeks ago we left Point Pleasant without tents or transportation, except that of the back. We marched fifteen miles the first day. We were compelled to use the rails of a hot rebel farmer, it was so cold. We built large fires and slept around them, but not very warm. * * We marched every day until Friday. This night, dark as it was, we perilously marched over hills and hollows, and stumps and rocks. It was cold and dark, and we were not permitted to talk above a whisper. * * We reached the enemy's camp to find it deserted. * * We have had one-third rations for two weeks. * * Hard business. * * The nearer they come to killing me, it seems, the better I like it.

Nov. 9, 1862. *Cotton Hill, Va.* * * Out all night and 'snowing all the time. Very cold this morning. * * In a snap we cut limbs of brush and propped them up for shelter for fifteen or twenty, building large fires in front. These the boys call boars' nests, bearing a strong resemblance to a hog bed. * * Battles have been fought all around It is the place where our forces tried to capture Floyd.

Nov. 18, 1862. *From Camp Fredrick, Va.* Dear parents. * * You have no idea how much good it does me to hear from home and Burch at the same time. * * Uncle Sam owes me $51, and when paid I will send it home. I want something to show when I get home, for God knows that if anybody earns his money it is the private soldier. You write that you have hard times feeding sixty hogs and gathering the corn, but your work done, you have a house and a good fire for warmth with a table filled with plenty, a bed to sleep in. I get up from the ground at 5:30 A. M., call the roll, get a cup of coffee and a hard cracker, sling my knapsack and accoutrements, and start upon the mountain march of twenty-five miles, and then throw myself on the ground (wet or dry), with a thin blanket for cover. * * Poor Jack Foraker is about gone up with the rheumatism * * I sometimes think it is no use to fight any longer when such men as —— ——, (a noted northern rebel) is allowed to live in Hillsboro.

1863.

January 22, 1863, *Camp Rosecrans, Va.* How did Burch (his brother) get along in the recent great battle? I learn he was on Gen. Rosecran's staff, and was riding over the field when the bullets flew thickest. He

always was a lucky fellow at home. I saw five shots fired from up on the
hill above our camp in a minute. The long roll was beat, and then you
ought to have seen your Ben. . . . .

January 30, 1863, Steamer Express. I send you $60, to use the best you
can; if your Ben never gets to his earthly home do what you please with it,
Company A is without a captain, but Ben Foraker will never ask for a
place. I have done my duty always, and have done nothing in the army
I would not have done at home. I know I have friends and, what is above
all, a clear conscience. . . .

Nashville, Tenn., Feb. 8, 1863. I must tell you of our fight the day we
reached Ft. Donnelson. The Eighty-third Illinois was attacked by about
7,000 rebels and artillery. They fought from 2:30 P. M. to 10 when we
came up with the gun-boats and immediately opened out on them, and
they "skeddadled." The next day I saw many dead rebels. Ah! To
know how dreadful war is you must see it yourself. At home you may
talk of the horrors of the field of battle and its wounded and dying, but to
realize, you must see it. Terrible is the responsibility and criminality of
those begining a war, and such a war, to build a nation on the corner-stone
of slavery. . . . .

March 6, 1863. . If I am not careful, my debts will consume my wages.

March 24, 1863. . Marched all day and night and next day. . . Have
not slept two hours since we left and got into camp. Hard soldiering. . .

Camp near Carthage, Tenn,, March 29, 1863. . Awaiting rebels, he
writes : No fire was allowed, and so sleep was out of the question, the
night being bitter cold. We awaited the coming morn' for relief from our
suffering. . . The rebels had disappeared. . . We marched twelve miles
and then halted until sundown, and then marched till midnight, halting
one hour and a half. . . Marched and scouted until next midday. . .
Never was a boy gladder to get into camp than your son. My feet were in
a blister, and every bone in my body was as sore as if beaten with a ham-
mer. . , Yet I could only be satisfied in the service of my country, and
as long as there is an armed rebel in the land, and a demand for men, I
shall be on the field. . . There are some wishing our glorious Republic
and her armies no good luck. Between them and me there can be no
friendship. These men who would corrupt and demoralize our army have
the bitter contempt of the soldiers. I shall do what duty calls for. If it
should be my lot to fall by disease, or on the field of battle, I ask no sympathy from the enemies of my country. . . I like all my officers. . .

Camp near Carthage, Tenn., April 26, 1863. The longer I live the more
I become impressed with the worth of character. Since I have been in
the army I have lived right up to my duty. . . Major Glenn has been
really a father to me. I never had better friends at home than here.

. . . . . . Yours, BEN.

May 5, 1863. The prisoners say they have been drawing only quarter
rations for months, and no coffee, sugar or salt. . . They all cry "peace,"
and that they will agree to come back to the Union as it was; but this war
will not end until all realize this is a Nation, and for the colored as well as
the white man. . . .

May 17. Burch at home. Does he look like the same dear old Burch
that he used to? He wrote me you almost killed him with kindness. . .

Carthage, Tenn., May 27. MOTHER DEAR. * * You desire me to tell
you about Jimmy Elliott, and what he said upon dying. * * His talk was
most about his mother. He said he was willing to die, and was not afraid

of death. He felt it would be all right with him. * * Will there be a camp-meeting this fall ? * * Yours. BEN.

May 31. * * A leave of absence of four days to meet Burch [his brother] at Nashville. It will be a glorious old meeting, you may bet your life. * * I wish mother was here to go fishing with me. * * Wouldn't mother's eyes glisten if she was to haul out one of the largest fish of this region. . . . Ask mother if she remembers the time she and I went fishing at the big rock, at the head of 'Spargur's dam. I can see her throwing them out, as fast as I could take them off the hook and string them. I was not bigger than a pound of soap then. What a change in our family. . . . But enough of this ; it makes me sad. . . .

Murfreesboro, Tenn., June 13, 1863. If there is anything I despise it is a man holding a commission in the army and at the same time finding fault with everything the administration does to put down the rebellion. .

September 2. DEAR FATHER . . . I congratulate you in your becoming a captain of the Home Guards. If you want to know how to drill them, come down here, and bring a box of provisions along, and then I will hitch you in for about one week, and then you can go home with a good idea of the tactics. . .

Chattanooga, Tenn., Dec. 1, 1863. . . . Arrived just in time to engage in the fight. I found the regiment under arms. The army charged Missionary Ridge. Our brigade charged on double-quick over two miles and up an awfully steep mountain. I commanded two companies, A and B,— brave boys. I threw myself in front and told them to follow. They kept as pretty a line as I ever saw them make on drill. The rebs had two cross fires and a front one. They knocked us around. I reached the top of a hill without a scratch, but just as I leaped over their breast-works a large shell burst just before me. A small fragment of it put a hole in my cap, knocking it off my head. . . As soon as I got into the breast-works and the rebs began to fall back I commenced rallying my men. I had the company about formed when Capt. Curtis, Gen. Turchin's adjutant general, galloped up to me and complimented me . . I never wish to see another fight. It is an awful sight to see men shot down all around you as you would shoot a beef. . .

Dec. 11. There is a hospital in the rear of our camp. You can hear the wounded screaming all through the day. Legs, arms, and hands lie before the door. . . They are cutting off more or less every day. . . War sickens me. . . I have about thirty men left out of the one hundred and one we started with over a year ago. The regiment does not look the same. . . Come what will, I shall stick to the company if I die with it.

1864.

Ringold, Ga., March 6, 1864. Foraker writes of the enemy taking a stand upon a hill after being pursued. He says : "More skirmishers being called for, I was ordered out with my company. I met the gentlemen half way, and after pouring several decided volleys into his ranks, I prevailed on him to go back and let me have full possession. I regained all the ground lost, and kept it until relieved at 11 o'clock that night, though repeated charges were made on my line with a much larger number. * * Our regiment had done splendid fighting. * * Capt. Vickers is a very brave man. * * I have $200 to my credit. I owe brother Burch $35 ; credit him and discredit me with this amount.

Near Kingston, Ga., May 20, 1864. Within fifty-six miles of Atlanta. You have read of our fighting from May 7 to 17. We were under fire all day the 14th. . . The rebels commenced retreating last Sunday night, and we have been following them, fighting their rear-guard every day since. . . I write this letter within gun shot of the skirmish line. The sun is just rising above the tree-tops. If the rebels make a stand a bloody day's work will soon commence. . . My company stands up to the work like men. I wish no more honorable position than I now have.

South of Etowah River, May 25. Within forty-five miles of Atlanta. . . Awfully hard campaign. It requires all my strength and energy to endure it. . . . .
July 6. Ten miles from Atlanta. Going to have a hard fight. The enemy have their fortifications on the opposite bank of the river, and will make warm work for us in crossing; but cross we will one way or another. . . The fatigues and hardships of our campaign of sixty-one days, have reduced our thirty-four men to nineteen. . . . .
In the Field, Georgia, July 26, 1864. We are within two miles of Atlanta, the Gate-City of the South. . . War will end soon. . . I am not discouraged. I am only tired and worn out. Think of eighty days in the field under fire every day, and in a dozen heavy engagements besides. . . I can't compare myself to anything better than one of Jake Foraker's old horses about the time corn is laid by. . . . .
Atlanta, Nov. 6, 1864. Dear Brother Burch: Was relieved from duty at Marietta, by Lieut. Adams yesterday. Arrived here last night. Capt. Bachtell will accompany Gen. Sherman. He was ordered to select five of his best officers and transfer them Dept. Cumberland to Mil. Div. I was selected as one of the five. The rest of the corps are sent back to Chattanooga. . . . .

1865.

Savannah, Jan. 13, 1865. My Dear Father: A slight attack of the chills and fever, but am getting well. I am on duty in this city. . . Our next campaign will open in about a week. . . I wish I had my two horses at home. . . .
One letter to his father is marked "confidential." It begins: "You being more experienced in the world than myself, I come to you for advice . . . I have a chance for a cadetship at West Point. . . What say you? My strongest reason is that I am just the right age to get an education, and I can get one at West Point and still be in the army. If I don't go there I think I should go to school at some place. . . . Who will be the next President? Get a man who will not fear to make a draft.

I am tired of handling this thing with gloves. I say pitch in and wipe them out. We have the men and the means. So why not put a stop to this unnatural rebellion at once. . . . .

HIS ARMY LIFE.

His own speeches contain at times allusions to his army life. At Camp-fire, McCook Post, No. 30, G. A. R., April 28, 1881, Judge Foraker's topic was "The Soldier in Civil Life." He spoke of civil life furnishing the soldiers, of the dread of war through the north, of men giving up private affairs, business interests, and home and families; of repeated efforts at compromise; of the south regarding us as destitute of fighting qualities; of our finding what blood courses our veins and of our patriotism, of our grand army of a million, and of our men ready for every branch of service. He stated that a colonel, needing a locomotive engineer, announced to his regiment that any man able to run a locomotive should step out, and fifty men stepped to the front. He said :

"I remember that when Sherman, on his march from Atlanta to the sea, captured Milledgeville, which was then the capital of Georgia, our boys took possession of the State House, from which the Confederate Legislature had precipitately fled the day before, organized a mock legislature, elected officers, appointed committees, drafted a bill and enacted it into a law, repealing the ordinance of secession and putting the state back into the Union ; and did it all as creditably, showing as much ability, as could any legislative body especially selected for the purpose. . . Thus we see that there is strength in popular government, and that government of the people, for the people, and by the people is no longer an experiment, but an established and demonstrated fact."

The Judge noticed the spirit of alarm that a military despotism with a favorite general for dictator would subvert our constitution and suppress our liberties, or that the country would be filled with an army of idle prowlers. He said :

"The soldiers in civil life to-day, are to be found in every field of usefulness, every art, every science, industry, and profession—with only enough exceptions to prove the rule, wherever you find an ex-soldier, you find a good, industrious, representative citizen. And not only are they toiling in the humbler walks of life, but they are honoring themselves and their country in the highest. As legislators, judicial officers, governors of states and presidents of the United States, they contribute to all the departments of government."

NEW DEPARTURE.

August 26, *1872*, before the Grant and Wilson Club, of Hillsboro, Judge Foraker said: "For notwithstanding the new departures with which the Democracy have recently seen fit to edify themselves, and notwithstanding the nomination of the Chappaqua philosopher, there is absolutely no safety and security for this government, nor for republican institutions in general, the world over, but in the continuance of this government in the hands of the same men who saved it until every question of the war and every question that has grown out of the war, shall have been permanently settled on the side of the right.

MISSION RIDGE.

These new departures remind me of an incident of the battle of Mission Ridge,—an incident which I think I shall never forget. When we had pushed our lines up that rugged mountain side, until we had come within a few paces of the rebel trench at the top and when, as it was obvious to every one, we would in another minute sweep over their lines, bearing down everything that might stand in the way, I saw a rebel soldier thrust his musket out over their works and fire it at us, almost in our very faces, and then, jerking it back, threw it down into the ditch behind him, leap over to our side and run into our lines, crying out to us at the top of his voice for us not to shoot him, for he was a *Union* man, our friend, etc. Our lines opened and he passed through, and down that rugged mountain side to our rear something after the manner and style of a streak of greased lightning. It all happened in one-half the time I have occupied in relating it. I don't know that I have ever seen the gentleman since, nor do I know that I ever shall see him again, but I do know that I always have believed, and most likely always shall believe, that if, instead of passing him to our rear, as we did, our men had received him on the points of their bayonets and passed him into eternity, he would have gone up to the bar of God with a lie in his mouth. And yet, my friends, that rebel was doing just exactly what the Democracy are pretending to do. He was taking his new departure. But I did not believe then, and I do not believe now, that his professions of Unionism and friendship were sincere. They indicated a change of mind entirely too radical, too sudden, and suspicious in its character and surrounding circumstances. And as I have never believed that that rebel was taking any genuine departure, except such as he could take by means of his legs, so have I never had any faith whatever in these departures of the Democracy. And the reason why I have never had any such faith are the very same identical reasons why I disbelieved that rebel.

Here they come, many long years later than they ought to have come, to have been appreciated, and pledge themselves to maintain the Union. Yes. They wait till the war is over, till the Union has been preserved, till we are in a condition such as to render it a matter of but slight consideration whether they stand the one way or the other, and then they come forward with the pledge that they ought to have given the country in 1861. They in favor of the Union! What a great pity it is that they didn't find it out sooner! What a great pity it is that they did not see fit to come forward in 1861, and clasp hands across the little chasms that intervened between party organizations with the Union men of the country and pledge themselves before the whole world to so continue to stand to the end. It is a great pity because, had they done so, the war, if ever commenced at all, would have terminated long before it did. And, in that event, many brave and precious "boys" would not have gone down as they did in sacrifice. But, my friends, it is not only a great pity that they so neglected this important matter, it is also a gross crime. The blood of all such "boys" is upon the skirts of this Democratic party.'

RECORD OF SERVICE

At the reunion of the the 89th O. V. I., Sept. 20, 1869, at Hillsboro, Judge Foraker, among other good utterances, said on our battle-flag are entitled to be written the following facts:

"Two years and eleven months in the service; more than three thousand miles traveled, over one thousand seven hundred of which were performed on foot, with knapsack on the back and the enemy in the front."

Hoover's Gap, Chickamauga, Mission Ridge, Rocky Face Ridge, Resacca, Kenesaw Mountain, Peach Tree Creek, Utoy Creek, Jonesboro', Atlanta,

Savannah, and Bentonville, are the battles, leaving unmentioned as too insignificant to be taken into consideration at least fifty such skirmishes as Phillipi, Rich Mountain, Scarey Creek, and Carnifex Ferry, which, in the beginning of the war, when they were fought, were thought to be great battles. And these are the *glorious* inscriptions which we are entitled to write upon our flag.

EIGHT HUNDRED FALLEN.

Next comes the recital of the *most terrible* price at which they were *purchased*. NEARLY 800 FALLEN! For, starting out with more than a thousand as hearty, strong, noble and patriotic men as ever obeyed a country's call, we returned to Camp Dennison at the close of the war numbering only 231, rank and file; and among them all there could scarce be found a corporal's guard who could not show where at least one bullet of the enemy had struck them. Not all of these 800 missing had fallen in battle, it is true, nor perhaps the half of them, for with us, as with all soldiers, the exposures and privations and over-fatigues were more destructive than the enemy's bullet. But whether they had languished and breathed their last on the couch in the hospital; or whether finally obtaining a discharge or furlough and reaching home, their pure spirits bade farewell to their tenements of clay, and winged their heavenward flight from among tender and weeping friends; or whether, as was the almost indescribably sad fate of so many of our brave boys, their bodies were wasted and their deaths hastened by a barbaric starvation in the still more barbaric prison pens of the South, far from friends, without even a shelter over them, denied the slightest attention and even the kindness of a decent burial; or whether the messenger of Death found them on the lonely picket and upon an ever-to-be-unknown spot, poured out their warm life's blood to sanctify, hallow and to make holy; or whether souls went up to God from amid the dust and smoke and shot and thunder of battle: it matters not. All must be alike enumerated in our mortality list; for all alike, though in so many different forms, fell victims to the same great cause. All alike, living sacrifices upon their country's alter, that their country might live.

A PLEDGE OF FRIENDSHIP.

And now my comrades: we who were spared in this terrible havoc; we who stood, while so many of our number prematurely went down unto the dust of death; we, who were permitted to survive the battles, the marches, the toils, the exposures, and all the other hardships and dangers incident to a soldier's life; we, who were of that fortunate few who were so highly favored as to be allowed to return home again, and enjoy in the bosom of families and in the midst of our friends that peace which our sacrifices and valor had achieved; we, who have all this to be thankful for, have gathered ourselves together to-day, not for the purpose of parade and glitter and show, but only that we may again stand in each other's presence and look upon each other's faces; that we may again clasp each other's hand, and while recalling and recounting the trials and dangers which we shared and passed through in common, have a recommingling of souls, and a refreshing and renewing of that friendship which, of all other friendships, is pre-eminently the first. And. this, the anniversary day of Chickamauga, is certainly a most appropriate time for our purpose; for, although duty called me elsewhere at the time, so that I do not have the honor of having participated in the engagement, yet, in common with every other member of the regiment, whether present or not, I can not but feel a glow of pride tingle down my cheek when I recall the heroic manner in which, from the beginning till the end of the fight, you battled almost to annihilation against most fearful odds, and finally, rather than desert your position, or yield an inch of ground, you yielded up that which is next dearest to life itself—*your own liberty.*

THE LAND OF THE FREE.

And it is because this day was one of such great disaster, as well as great glory, that we do well to so emphatically remember it as to make it our anniversary upon which to come together and repledge our friendship, and return our thanks to our Almighty Father, through whose omnipotent care we were saved harmless from the ravages by which so many of our most gallant officers and bravest men were swept from among us into eternity. But the preservation of our lives is not the only nor the great reason why we should to-day give thanks.

It is an unworthy selfishness that would prompt us to rejoice for no better reason than that the storms and dangers of war should have passed over and left us to bask, unharmed, in the sunshine of peace and the security of victory. Let us rejoice that our lot should have been cast in the day and land when and where the opportunity was afforded us of becoming the instruments, in the hands of a Divine Providence, with which to perform a work of such lasting benefit, not only to the present generation of mankind, but to those of all the ages which are to hereafter follow us. Yes, let the joy of our hearts be, that we can to-day recall that when the dark hour of peril and great responsibility came upon us, we were equal to the emergency and met it like men. That, unlike the many, who, under equal obligations with us, to the lasting disgrace of themselves and their innocent children after them, not only miserably, but most criminally, failed, we took our lives in our hands and went forth and stood as a wall of fire between the institutions of our Government and that enemy which, seeking the country's overthrow, were working the destruction of the country's people; and that in the performance of this duty we not only saved from destruction the works of our fathers and founders, but in addition brought them to a much higher perfection, by wiping out that great stigma, which, so long as it remained and received the recognition and protection of our laws, retarded our development and corroded our morals by giving the lie to our boasted professions that here was "the land of the free and the home of the brave;" where the oppressed and down-trodden of every country and clime could find a *welcome,* a refuge, and a *home.*

FORAKER AT HOME AND SCHOOL.

Before Ben Foraker was nineteen years of age he was mustered out of the U. S. service,—June 14, 1865.

The war over, the Union preserved, the slave at liberty, and young Foraker returned to farm, mill and school, studying at Salem, Ross County. He was two years at the Wesleyan University, at Delaware, Ohio, and then went to Cornell University, graduating in the classical course, July 1, 1869, and in its first class.

With his limited means he was not only assiduous in his academ-

3

ical studies, but at the same time he was also a student at law. A dear friend and class-mate says that not only did he study and read under high pressure, but on plain fare, at times boarding himself and thus reducing his expenses to the minimum that he might eke out his scanty means and finish his entire course.

He went to Cornell from the University, with a letter from the Rev. Dr. Merrick, the then President, honorably dismissing him and certifying to his character as a student and as a gentleman, "In all respects entirely unexceptionable."

His literary reputation at college may be somewhat determined by the subjects for essays assigned him. His essay upon "Macbeth," published in the Collegian, is modest and yet marks the thinker. The student, Foraker, asks why we should read Shakspeare? He refers to human nature all around, as well as in the plays of the bard, and that Duncans and Macbeths stalk over the land in broad daylight, and that were there fewer men with just sense enough to quote Shakspeare, and no more than to render themselves ridiculous by tentative efforts at imitation, our writing and oratory would be advanced in respectability. Foraker's analysis of Macbeth would do credit to an older essayist.

In 1869 he was elected as the proper person to write to Senator Sumner to deliver an address at Cornell, and to receive the great Massachusetts Senator upon his arrival.

Foraker is the only man who graduated first in the army, and then took college honors. As for his youth, "one ages rapidly," said Napoleon, "on the battle-field."

Major White, of Springfield, thus writes of his record at college:

"He was a recognized leader among the students; probably because of his long military experience before entering the college, as he came fresh from the battle-field to Delaware. In his studies he was one of the most exhaustive students I ever knew, as he always took up a branch of study with a view of getting the most complete and comprehensive ideas on it."

"He was probably the best debater in the college. He was a prominent member of the Zetegathean Society, a literary society of the college, and was one of the most prominent members in it. Foraker was always chosen to represent the Zetegatheans in any debate or contest in public, and in any literary or forensic contest with a rival society."

"From the time of entering, while not neglecting his literary studies, much attention was given to the study of the law, and his time, study and energy were directed toward this end. He was foremost in organizing a moot court and mock trials, and invariably acted as Judge, thus giving a prophecy of his future career."

"Foraker was not of the kind to make anecdotes. He was a lively, determined, studious young man, with a life object in view, and an indomitable will to obtain it. He was little inclined to joking, and was always earnest and serious. In the college tricks and pranks he took no part."

"He was head of his classes, and to show how great was his proficiency in his studies, I will simply state that he went from the Sophomore Class in Delaware, directly to the Senior Class at Cornell, thus jumping a class. He followed the classical course at both universities, but made an especial effort in all branches having a legal bearing or tendency."

"He was extremely popular with both pupils and professors. His studious, earnest bearing endeared him to all, and made him one of the most popular young men in the whole university."

Judge Vernon, of the Clinton County *Republican*, says :

"Foraker and myself were members of the same literary society while at college. In the debates, whatever side had Foraker, was almost certain to win. He was always a sure, strong fellow."

THE FLAG CAN'T COME DOWN.

A college mate at Delaware and lawyer at Dayton recalls an incident that well illustrates the effect of Captain Foraker's presence. Upon the college campus was a flag-staff brought from Camp Dennison, and erected at the expense of the students, who were Republicans almost to a man. After some election or national event, distasteful to the Democrats, the flag was hoisted to the top of the staff, by way of a glorification. In the afternoon of that day it was rumored that some Democratic citizens, not students, would lower the flag or cut down the pole that night. The boys arranged to have a couple of watchmen, and upon any hostile demonstration the chapel bell was to be rung. Sure enough, late at night some burly fellows made their appearance upon the campus and blustered about what they were going to do. While one watchman parleyed with them the other ran to the bell-rope, and in ten minutes the campus was black with students. Foraker was there, and although only a freshman or sophomore, and by no means one of the oldest students, they all instinctively turned to him for leadership. He confronted the disturbers, addressed them a few decided words in a dignified way, and told them that that flag would never be lowered nor the pole cut down. They departed. The pole was not thereafter molested. The circumstance shows the quality of Foraker, and the estimate in which he was held by his companions, and by his political opponents. When Foraker said the pole should not be cut down and the flag should not be lowered, all knew that Foraker meant to resist the insult to the flag with his whole physical power—that it meant fight to the death.

MEN AND PHI KAPPA PSI.

We extract some choice periods from an address of J. B. Foraker, graduate member of New York Alpha, before the Phi Kappa Psi Fraternity, Columbus, Ohio, August 19th and 20th, 1874 :

".... You are here as the representatives of the active working members of the fraternity! . . Only they who have experienced it can know how sweetly, grandly, and proudly will resurrect themselves in one's memory, bringing peace to the troubled mind, teaching its ever noble duty where the way is not plain, and lending strength for victory when the soul is tempted, those quiet, modest, but diamond-like words, *"Never forget that you are a member of the Phi Kappa Psi fraternity."* '

* * * * * * * * . *

"Your duty is not a mere college pastime. Its objects are higher,— the symmetrical developement of our whole nature. It means men, men in the highest sense of the word, men who will depart from college to the battles of life with honesty of purpose, with appreciation of right, and with a power for work that will render the world better. Hence, be dili- gent, earnest, brave, honest, and God-fearing — a credit to yourselves, an honor to your society, a gain to the world — . . making the mind brighter, the heart warmer, and the soul nobler as you pass on to eternity.

* * * * * * * * *

It is plausibly argued that the world is full of bad people, that lying, cheating, and evil generally are prevalent, and therefore 'You must fight the devil with fire,' that success must come by the use of like instrument- alities. Is this not generally an apology for misguided conduct?"

* * * * * * * * *

"When Sir Francis Bacon bartered away the high honor of the great office of Law Chancellor of England, humiliation and disgust sickened every true heart of that proud realm. . . . But when the strong arm of the people was found sufficient, despite his mighty genius and influence to humble this great man, and strip him of the accumulations of his robber- ies, confidence in humanity revived and grew stronger, demonstrating not the retrogression of mankind, but the abuse of trust by one poor, weak public servant. . So with the discovery and punishment of our own faithless servants. . . Let us take cheer from the manifestations of vir- tue by which the people turn their backs upon their idols, rebuking sin and encouraging righteousness."

After giving much useful advice the Judge said :

"You may not thus gather wealth — you may not gather fame, but your mind will know a serenity, your heart a sunshine, and your soul an assur- ance, compared with which all the riches and honors of the world are ver- iest baubles. Not because you shall be free from storms of trouble, but because you shall have the anchor of safety. . . You may be in ad- vance of many as to your opinions. Don't seek to avoid censure and crit- icism and to destroy your self-respect in an outward approval of the errors of the many. Boldly and unhesitatingly maintain your own sentiments. The most disgusting, demoralizing, and discouraging feature of entire po- litical systems is the abominable demagoguery of truckling to popular sen- timent."

* * * * * * * *

LET POLITICS ALONE.

"Let politics alone" is sounded in the ears of the college graduate. . . In this Democratic country of ours every man is charged with a voice in the Government. . . If the wicked are put in power, and disaster over- take us, will it be a sufficient excuse for the good man that he takes no part in politics? . . We must not sleep on guard and be criminally un- mindful of our highest duty. . . Have all to do with politics, both understanding and controlling. . . Our surest safety in politics lies in the exercise of honesty and intelligence in the formation and presentation of public questions."

DISFRANCHISEMENT OF STUDENTS.

The Judge in 1868, himself a student, gave to the press his views of the disfranchisement of students by the Democratic legislature.

"There are about four hundred students attending this university (Delaware), about two hundred are voters. Not more than twenty of all are Democrats. The remainder are unqualified Union men. I do not know that this is the case with *all* the colleges of the state. It is so with most; and I presume the Legislature thought it so with all, for in their very great *wisdom* and exceeding *patriotism*, they have thought best to *disfranchise* us, while here as students, hoping thereby to cheat a few Republicans out of their votes, discourage education, and retard progress and enlightenment, the most deadly enemies with which the Democratic party has ever had to contend.

"But, aside from this view of the matter, the law is certainly one of very great injustice and hardship to the students of both parties. For why should not the student enjoy the same rights that are extended to any other description of temporary inhabitant? The *clerk* and the *mechanic* have but to remain here the time required by the statute, and their right to exercise the elective franchise becomes unquestionable, whether they are here temporarily or permanently. And so it should be with all classes of persons, and any enactments to the contrary are uncalled for and unjust. So we must pronounce this act, when we take it by itself; but when we couple with it the circumstances and facts to which it owes its existence, it becomes particularly offensive, and our disapproval ripens into contempt for a body of men who are so lost to duty, lost to honor, and lost to conscience, as thus to legislate away the dearest of all American rights—the ballot."

AS A LAWYER.

He entered the law office of Judge James Sloane, then practicing in Cincinnati. He was admitted to the bar of Hamilton County in the fall of 1869, and at once began practice, with no influential friends in the city and without the usual aid of membership in some secret or social club

"Slow rises worth, by poverty depressed."

Thus it was with him for a season; but his genial manners, indomitable energy, great ability, and stern Christian integrity eventually secured him practice, in every court, from that of the local magistrate to the supreme court of the United States.

Hon. Ben. Eggleston says it was but a short time before the people of that great city saw that he was not an ordinary man; that there was something in and about him more than there was in ordinary young men.

Judge Foraker, at the beginning of his law course, wrote, June 1870, an essay for a Wilmington journal, in which (unintentionally) he gave his personal views of the law as a profession and the spirit upon which he entered upon its duties. He had no apology for the "infamous Jeffries," nor for "Noy, who by his technical quibbling evaded and delayed the ends of justice;" nor for "Eldon, who perverted his legal knowledge and powers to prevent more good than any other man had accomplished in a life time." He claimed and felt (and thus entered upon his work) that "the work of the lawyer is in harmony with, and part of the great labor of carrying humanity forward;" that his work is not only of pecuniary benefit to mankind," but that the "lawyer's great work, properly viewed, is most closely allied to that of the clergy;" that lawyers should check and not promote the "perturbations of society;" that they should be leaders in contests for truth, liberty, and progress, and be ever on the side of the oppressed.

HIS MARRIAGE.

October 4, 1870, Judge Foraker, with the memory of a blessed paternal home, married Miss Julia A. P. Bunday, a daughter of Hon. Hezekiah S. Bunday, of Jackson, Ohio; the intimate friend of Lincoln, and a member of Congress in the most eventful period of our history. This lady he met while she was a scholar at the Ohio Wesleyan Female College, at which she graduated in 1868, and where she was noted for her high literary attainments.

God has blessed this sacred union with one son and three daughters.

Mrs. Foraker often urged her husband to prepare an *autobiography*. The Judge wrote the preface thus :

"I never liked the idea of *autobiographies*. For a man to write disparagingly of himself cannot be commendable. "It is a mean bird that fouls its own nest." If one's career deserves disparagement, there will be others to afford it. If not, it is at least well enough, if not better, to let it go unwritten.

On the other hand, if praise is merited, others should sound it. To praise oneself will appear egotistic—no matter how deserved. To avoid both disparagement and praise is difficult, if not well-nigh impossible.

It might be thought these objections could be avoided by a mere naked statement of facts, but that is not really true, since the mere statement of any given act must carry with it the idea that, accordingly as its nature may be, the author suffers it to redound to his credit. Entertaining such views, it is in the nature of an unpleasant task that I enter upon this short work, and yet I undertake it, contradictory as it may seem, in another sense, with very great pleasure. I do it at the request of a loving, admiring and devoted wife; a wife who by ten years of fidelity, affection and devotion to every duty, and by four as bright and beautiful children as ever graced any union, has merited and won for herself all the confidence and love that belongs to the several and hallowed offices of wife and mother. These statements must be my apology for these pages.

The Judge wrote a few lines and never resumed the task.

FORAKER AT HOME.

Our public men should not only be moral and upright men, but men who appreciate home life and are examplars of family, as of patriotic sentiment. What would our nation be without its homes?

Upon entering the home of Judge Foraker, with the home-spirit, and not with that of impertinent intrusion, in lifting the purple curtains where his weary brain reposes, we find a true home, a true husband, and a true father. We exercise no distasteful scrutiny; but, we can not but see a true religious and American home. The country more and more demands of our statesmen that they erect for themselves, pure, virtuous homes.

The Judge has no sympathy with the sentiment or the law that destroys the individuality of the wife, or which awards greater punishments to a woman for the same vice, or which classes women with infants and idiots; yet he values the intellectual filtering through the moral nature, giving power, maintaing virtue, exercising that subtle influence which makes every moment a seed-time of future good, and finding scope for mind and heart in the education of the children. He esteems the wife as companion, lover, friend and counsellor, having her especial duties as he has his—a division of labor.

JUDGE OF SUPERIOR COURT.

In April, 1879, he was elected a Judge of the Superior Court of Cincinnatti. He held this office for three years. The kind of record he made is best shown by the expressions elicited by his resignation. One decision selected at random out of the many that have been published will illustrate his logic and style of expression:

SUPERIOR COURT OF CINCINNATI.

GENERAL TERM, JANUARY 1882.

MARGARET R. POOR, Plaintiff.

vs.

SARAH S. SCANLAN AND MAURICE J. SCANLAN, Her Husband.

Foraker, J.:

This case was reversed upon the evidence. It is an action for rent. From the pleadings and the evidence it appears that March 1st, 1857, the plaintiff, being then the owner thereof, leased a certain lot on the north side of Third street in the city of Cincinnati, to George Selves, for ninety-nine years, renewable forever. The certificate of acknowledgement of the lease was not written on the same sheet of paper that the lease was written upon, but on a separate sheet attached to the paper the lease was written upon, by a common paper fastener. All parties seem, however, to be ignorant of this fact until after this suit was brought. Selves held possession of the premises under the lease, paying the rents reserved therein: $250 every quarter, until his death in 1862. When he died he left a will by which he devised to his widow Sarah Selves, now Sarah S. Scanlan, the defendant herein, all his real estate for life. She elected to take under his will, and at once took possession of this leasehold estate. She remained in possession continously until after this action was commenced, paying the rents reserved according to the covenants of the lease, until June 1, 1878, when she refused to pay the quarter's rent then falling due, and offered to surrender the premises, which offer was not accepted. She had not paid anything since. In 1869 she married her co-defendant, Maurice J. Scanlan, who, jointly with her, has occupied and used the premises since, until they quit possession in 1881.

This action was commenced in 1879, to recover four installments of rent that had become due, amounting to $1,000. The petition simply alleged that there was due the plaintiff, from Sarah S. Scanlan and Maurice J. Scanlan, for rent of the said premises, $1,000, and prayed for judgment against the defendants. Nothing was said, either in the style of the case or the body of the petition, about the defendants being husband and wife. No reference was made to the lease, and there was no allegation that the wife had a separate estate. The case stood upon this petition and a general denial filed thereto, by the defendants, when it came on for trial. The facts above mentioned appearing, the plaintiff was allowed to re-file an amended petition which she had previously filed and withdrawn, in which the facts above stated, except as to the defective acknowledgment of the lease, were fully set out, together with allegations that the wife had a separate estate, followed by a prayer for judgment and appropriate relief. The defendants excepted to the re-filing of this amended petition, and thereupon answered, denying all the allegations of the amended petition, except that George Selves occupied the premises at his death, that Mrs. Scanlan was the devisee of all his real estate for life, and that she entered into and held possession of the premises in question until 1881, and that she married Scanlan in 1868, also that she held for life, under the will of Selves, the real estate described in the petition, as her separate estate. Defendants claim that the amended petition ought not to have been allowed, because a departure.

It is not pretended that defendants were surprised or placed at any dis-advantage by it. The provision of our code on this subject is that such amendments may be made when in furtherance of justice, and when they do not·substantially change the claim or defense. Section 5114. In the case of *Spice vs. Steinruck*, 14th O. S., 213, it was held that this did not refer to the *form* of the remedy, but only to the general identity of the claim, and, consequently, that it was permissible, as was done in that case, to so amend the petition as to change the action, which was to re-cover damages for a malicious prosecution, to support which malice and want of probable cause had to be shown, to an action for damages for an illegal arrest, to sustain which it was not necessary to show malice or want of probable cause, but only a *void* process. The amendment in this case certainly does not change the claim that is made in the petition. At most it but changes the form. It can scarcely be said to fairly do even that. It is really nothing more than a statement of the facts of which we have the naked legal effect set forth in the petition, with some allegations about a separate estate, which according to our view of the case, are only so much surplusage.

Considering the case upon its merits, there are two general propositions relied upon by the defendants. In the first place it is claimed, that because Mr. Scanlan was the devisee of this leasehold only for life, she took less than the whole term, and she was consequently a sub-lessee, and not an as-signee, and if but a sub-lessee, not liable to the lessor for want of privity of estate.

For a second defense it is insisted that the defendant, Mrs. Scanlan, has done no act to authorize her separate estate to be charged.

Either of these propositions would be sufficient for the defendants if it could be applied to this case. But in our opinion, neither one has applica-tion.

The first has not, because the instrument intended for a lease to Selves was invalid, as such, by reason of the acknowledgment being written on on a separate sheet of paper. Winkler vs. Higgins, 9 O. S., 599. It did not pass the term to Selves. It was, consequently, at most but an equita-ble lease, giving him a right to occupy and enjoy the premises upon the terms and conditions named in it, and binding him, as upon personal cov-enant, to comply with is terms and conditions, so long as he remained in possession. Bridgeman vs. Wells, 13 Ohio, 43. This equitable right was all that passed by the devise. And this right and defendant took without assuming his personal covenant. Her undertaking was by an implied con-tract to pay for her use and occupation, so long as she enjoyed the same, according to the terms of the lease. This contract was between her and the lessor; hence their was privity of contract at least,

The second proposition would be unanswerable, if the plaintiff's right to recover a judgment depended upon a right to charge Mrs. Scanlan's sep-arate estate upon such a contract entered into during coverture. For we fully agree with the claim of her counsel, that in such a case it must be shown that she intended to charge her separate estate, and that such in-tention was relied upon. But, in our judgment, this is not such a case. This is merely an action to recover a personal judgment, and whether or not such a judgment shall be rendered, does not depend upon, and is not affected by, the question whether or not she at all has a separate estate.

Mrs. Scanlan was a *feme sole* when she took possession of these premises.

She was therefore competent to contract, and as we have seen, did, by implication, contract to pay, according to the terms of the lease, so long as she remained in possession. Her continued possession, after marriage, as well as before, must be referable to her original entering, and must have been therefore in pursuance of the contract to which we have alluded as thereby made for her by operation of law. Especially do we think so in view of the fact that she took possession for life, and hence did not have occasion to periodically consider, whether or not she would continue there. This being true, she held the premises at the time the rents accrued, for which she is now sued, under a contract, which the law made for her when she took possession, and which was in force when she married her codefendant, whereby she was obliged to pay the same. It is upon that contract that this action is based: a contract therefore substituting at the time of marriage; not made during coverture, but before.

This view is not affected by the fact that her occupation, after marriage, was jointly with her husband, since her interest and rights in the property under our statute, section 3108, remained her separate estate.

The case is, therefore, properly stated, an action against husband and wife, to recover rents that have become due, during coverture, upon a contract made by the wife before marriage, and existing at the time of marriage. At common law, marriage made the husband liable for the existing obligations of his wife. But in all actions against him to enforce them, she must be joined as a co-defendant, without regard to whether she had a separate estate or not. *Drew vs. Thorne*, Aleyn, 72, 7 Term, Rep., 348. If, therefore, we had no statute on the subject, this action would lie against the defendant for a money judgment.

In such case however, *i. e.* if there were no statute, the separate property of the wife could not be taken to satisfy the judgment. But in such actions we have instead of a common law rule that the *wife* must be joined with the husband, sec. 4996, of rev. statues, which require the husband to be joined with the wife. And instead of the wife's separate estate being exempt from liability to be taken to satisfy the judgemnt we have it expressly made liable by section 3110, which provides that "the separate property of the wife shall be liable to be taken for any judgement rendered in an action against husband and wife, upon a cause existing against her at their marriage, etc."

The language of this section has been changed somewhat since the case of Westerman *vs.* Westerman, 25 O. S., 500, where it was constructed to mean that the wife's separate property was not only liable to be taken in such case, but that as between her, and her husband's property, it was primarily liable, but the change has only made it more apparent that the legislative intent agreed with the construction of the Court.

Our conclusion is that this is an action against Mrs. Scanlan and her husband on a contract obligation of hers, existing at their marriage, that it is immaterial whether she intended to charge her separate estate or not, and that judgment should be rendered for the plaintiff; Jas. H. Perkins and D. H. J. Holmes, attorneys for defendants.

THE TRUE MAN.

We desire not to study Joseph Benson Foraker as a lawyer, soleier, or scholar, but to discover the man in the conduct of the lawyer, judge, soldier, and scholar. We study his briefs and charges and speeches to see how he links himself with broad humanity, to discover why men and women, citizens and soldiers trust him, and honor him. Thus we present the remarkable address that Judge Foraker delivered in memoriam before the District Court at Hillsborough, Ohio, upon the death of Judge Sloan, with whom Judge Foraker was formerly a law student.

JUDGE SLOANE.

Among his embarassments in delivering the address he said, "that Judge Sloan was unlike any man of his acquaintance."

"On account of some of his peculiar traits of character, I know him to be a greatly misunderstood man by a majority, I think, of the people who professed to be acquainted with him. And knowing him to have been thus misunderstood, I fear there may be those who will regard at least a part of what I shall say in praise of his character as mere empty and fulsome eulogy, instead of earnest and honest testimony.

I have no desire, or interest either, to speak in this matter aught save the strictest truth; and I know that he for whom I speak had so much truth in his heart, that he would utterly despise the slightest deviation therefrom, no matter how much that deviation might favor his memory in the estimation of men.

Therefore, I feel perfectly free, as well as conscientiously obligated, to say here to-day, as I have frequently said to the deceased in his lifetime, that there were certain striking features in his outward character that were objectionable, in the most serious sense of the word; for I considered them immoral and pernicious in their influences.

But for these things Judge Sloane is not answerable to us. That settlement must take place between him and that highest, wisest, and kindest Judge of all. . . . Let us remember that humane injunction of the Savior, "Judge not, that ye be not judged."

It was my fortune to know Judge Sloane well. I knew him for a number of years, and in a variety of relations. I think the majority of even this community, where he lived and died, never knew him except as I first knew him, and by all such Judge Sloane was not really known at all; for I first knew him only as a great, intellectual, legal giant, upon whom, when he went forth into public places, I, in common with others, was at liberty to look; and, if he chanced to pass my way, the compliments of the day might perhaps be deferentially exchanged. Closer than this I felt that I dared not, and I know that I desired not, to go; for there seemed to be a kind of Ishmaelitish coldness and bitterness about the man that rendered him uninviting to all except his personal friends, who knew him well, or such as might stand in need of his splendid talents.

In short, as I have already stated, I thought him only a cold, selfish, ambitious, intellectual giant; and had I never come closer to Judge Sloane, his loss would not now concern me much; for I have long since learned that there are giants in *these* as well as in *those* days, and that the places of giants simply are easily supplied.

FRIEND, PRECEPTOR, ASSOCIATE.

But I shall always be glad that it was within God's providence that I should know Judge Sloane better. His great abilities as a lawyer led me to sufficiently subordinate my objections to him personally to enable me to take a place as a student in his office. My association and connection with him, in some manner, was uninterrupted from that time until the day of his death. And I can say now, that in all the relations of a friend, a preceptor, as associate, and as opposing counsel, I have ever found him to be the very soul of honor.

He was the very body of truthfulness itself. I don't believe the man ever told a lie in his life. And when I remember how my daily experience teaches me that "the world is given to lying," I feel that absolute truthfulness is a rare and an ordinary virtue to be ascribed to any man.

But Judge Sloane was not simply a *truthful* man. He was as honest.

I don't mean that Judge Sloane was honest merely in money matters. The country is full of people who pay back all they borrow, and pay for all they buy, and take not, unlawfully, that which belongs to another. There are a thousand reasons why a man should be honest in these respects, and a thousand reasons why a man deserves no credit for such honesty.

Judge Sloane was honest in that higher, and better, and *braver* sense of the word. He was honest in the sense that honesty is the equivalent to truthfulness. There was no sham about him—no hypocrisy—no deception —no false pretense—no borrowed capital—no sailing under false colors. Whatever he pretended or appeared to be, that he was. If he manifested a spirit of friendliness toward any one, it was a genuine spirit, and the person toward whom it was manifested could rely on it to the fullest extent. And on the other hand, if he disliked any one, if was a genuine dislike, but the person disliked need have no difficulty in learning the facts in the case.

In other words, whatever he was that he was earnestly, fearlessly, and outspokenly, and whatever he believed, he believed earnestly, and what he didn't believe earnestly he didn't believe at all. He was no reed to be shaken by the wind.

Judge Sloane was also a kind and generous man. I do not mean kind and generous to the rich, for that would be easy for any man to be; nor to his equals, nor to the well-to-do classes—from all which sources he might reasonably have expected some benefit in return. Nor do I mean that he was kind and generous in public places, where his acts of kindness and generosity would be seen and known of all men. But he was kind and generous in a way that showed his kindness and generosity to be genuine. He was kind and generous privately rather, and to the poor and lowly, from whom he could not possibly expect anything in return.

HIS CHARITY.

I well remember, and shall never forget an incident that occurred in his office at Cincinnati, while I was a student with him. Hardly a day passed witnout from one to a half-dozen beggars coming into the office, with their various stories of poverty and destitution.

The city of Cincinnati cares and provides well for all who are really needy, and on this account it is rarely the case that any one who knows it, as Judge Sloane did, gives anything at all to that class of mendicants.

It was to my surprise, therefore, that day after day I observed that he never refused a single application, but patiently and kindly listened to the appeals of all, and gave something to every single one.

One day I ventured to call his attention to the matter, and to suggest that perhaps he was being imposed upon. There was a perfect sermon of genuine religion and Christianity in his reply, that, "he had long since come to the conclusion, that it was better to be imposed upon in many cases, than to turn away empty even one worthy applicant."

But Judge Sloane was kind in another respect. He was kind to the young practitioner. And standing here to-day, as in some measure the representative of the younger members of the bar, you will excuse me if I ask a special remembrance of this trait of his character. . . . .

It should not be any uncommon virtue, yet we all know that it too truly is. Every young man who starts in the profession of the law must encounter difficulties and perplexities, and troubles of various kinds. . .

. . When the country was imperiled and brave hearts were needed at the front, he was the first of all our citizens to appreciate the situation and to step forward with both his services and his blood. · . . .

Of Judge Sloane as a lawyer I shall say but little. We all know how he towered among us; and how his mind was exceptionally remarkable for its power of discernment, analysis, and logical reasoning. . . . .

. . We know, too, how, with an almost uncommon fidelity, he at all times maintained the interests of his clients. . . . But for that "grievous fault," for which he was continually "grievously answering," he would in all probability have risen to national importance. . . . .

When we consider the turbulent times through which we have just passed, the great fields of national usefulness that they presented, and the rich honors that have been therein gathered by others; and when we further consider his splendid abilities, his scrupulous honesty, and his unswerving patriotism, who can feel otherwise than that it was a genuine misfortune both to the country and himself, that Judge Sloane did not figure in national affairs. . . . .

. . . But regrets are vain. His life has been lived; his record is made. . . By his sad loss let us be freshly and impressively reminded of the importance of correctly living while we do live, of making the most of time while we have it, both for this world and eternity.

AN HONEST OFFICER.

In the fall of 1876, Judge Baxter, of the U. S. Circuit Court, appointed Foraker to the delicate and responsible position of Chief Supervisor of Elections for the Southern District of Ohio. Again he made a personal sacrifice of feeling and business in the interest of his country and party, and of the purity of the ballot. He administered its duties so fairly that even the Democrats, in their Congressional investigations, made record of his honorable integrity as the officer of the law.

Judge Foraker, by common consent, was agreed upon by men of all parties, and endorsed by the Judge for chief supervisor by reason of his purity, integrity, and courage, as " worthy, honorable and true in every respect, who would desire nothing but a free, fair, straightforward election, and as down on all fraud, and down on all men who undertake to cast an illegal vote, or import votes from any State to Ohio, or from any ward or precinct to any other."

It is remarkable that in the canvas to be hotly contested, and amid the anxieties of candidates and parties for victory, Judge.

Foraker was the only person upon whom all, Democrats and Republicans could harmonize. It is an enviable tribute to honest and moral worth.

In the spirit of eminent fairness, Judge Foraker, as chief supervisor, asked Mr. Sayler, as chairman of the Democratic elective and campaign committees, to present the names of Democrats as supervisors. He said that he desired to have "all parties fairly represented, and by only good, honest, representative men, who will perform their duties solely in the interest of an honest election, and without regard to partizan advantages."

In the course of the correspondence with the obstructives of the law to promote pure elections, Judge Foraker took occasion to declare that the government of the United States could not only protect itself against an armed rebellion, but could protect itself against fraud and abuse at the ballot-box. .

The character of Judge Foraker is seen in his instructions to his subordinate supervisors. After a minute examination of their duties and methods so as to cover almost every conceivable case, he declares that their duties are "to secure an honest, full and free expression of the voice of the people. This is of far greater importance than the success of any party or candidate. You are the representatives of all parties and all candidates, and your work is in the interest of the whole people—for law, order and good government. You will, therefore, carefully abstain from all electioneering, discussion and controversy."

Such an administrator of law may be safely trusted in any executive position.

Foraker was nominated for Judge of the Court of Common Pleas, in 1867, but was defeated by the notorious Eph. Holland frauds of that year. The confidence of the Republican Community in Judge Foraker was again evinced in his nomination for County Solicitor, in 1868. This was without his knowledge and against his wishes, but he served his party and his country, when he knew that he would suffer defeat.

RESIGNATION.

Upon the announcement in Cincinnati that Judge Foraker contemplated leaving the bench, the strongest remonstrances were made by the legal fraternity and by lay friends, without regard to party. They insisted upon his retaining the position, and the taking of a long vacation until his health had been regained ; that his health had been lost in public service and that the vacation was his right. But his sensitive nature would not permit his receiving the least portion of salary for which no current equiv-. alent was rendered. After the resignation had been forwarded to Columbus, telegrams were sent to the governor urging its non-acceptance. Among them were those from Hons. Force, Hoadley, Perry, Kettredge, and Warrington.

NO WORK, NO PAY. FORAKER'S MAXIM.

Mr. Eggleston thus describes his interview with Judge Foraker as to his resignation :

"No, Mr. Foraker, they [Democrats and Republicans of the bar] say they will not permit you to resign; that you must take a six month's vacation, and keep your seat. What do you think that earnest young man said? 'Why,' said he, 'Mr. Eggleston, it would look like stealing for me to take the salary and be absent from my duty; and I can not do it.'"

From many letters upon Judge Foraker's resignation we select but a few to furnish appreciatory extracts.

From Judge Harmon :

". . . Sorrow was the first feeling; and it still fills my mind. . . I can only say, God go with you wherever you go, and compensate me by many years of friendship for the few years of official companionship I am to lose. . . . In the three years we have spent together here I have come to love you as a brother. I long since passed the point of mere respect and admiration. I consider you as one of those friends a man rarely makes when he has reached our age—a friend who not only fills the romantic idea of youth, but meets the requirements of mature judgment. . . I am sad and lonely . . . Knowing it can not remain a secret, I mentioned it to some friends of the bar. The feeling is unanimous that the bench and bar sustain a great loss in your leaving the bench. They talk of petitioning you to reconsider, etc. . . Judge Hoadley and others have telegraped the governor . . ."

From Judge Worthington :

". . . I can not express my regret, and that of every member of the bar I have met and they have been many. If in one year of judicial service that opens before me I can gain the confidence and respect of the bar to one third of the extent that it has been given to you . . . I shall feel highly gratified."

Judge O'Connor, who expressed his regret at the resignation of Judge Foraker, and the cause of it, hoped that he would recall it, and take rest and travel ; that "the superior court is so advanced in work that absence would be without the slightest detriment to the public, or if at a slight disadvantage, the public loss would be nothing compared with its loss" if the resignation is persisted in. The Judge said:

"I know the feeling among the bar is unanimous that there would be irreparable injury in losing you from the bench; and they are also unanimous in wishing you to take the necessary rest and vacation. Therefore I hope you will regard these earnest wishes of your friends, the bar, and the public and withdraw your resignation. Do not hesitate on account of any idea of false delicacy about receiving your salary while absent from the court house. The public, not only would not so regard it, but would look upon it as the only proper course to take The public could far better afford to pay you many months salary than to lose your services, when you will, in all probability, be able to resume your duties, with all your ability, vigor, and usefulness, in the fall."

Judge Force telegraphed Judge Foraker from Washington City: "I have telegraphed the governor not to accept your resignation. Judge Harmon and I will keep up your work."

From an eminent lawyer of Cincinnati:

"... Your leaving will be a great public loss. . . I would comfort you in this hour of need and of peace. I can only lead you to Him who has said, 'Come unto me and I shall give you rest.'"

From another lawyer of Cincinnati:

"... I always found you to be the same good-hearted friend, trying to help every one."

The *Gazette*, (Cin.) April 12, 1882: "Judge Foraker has earned the admiration of the best practitoners at the bar by his promptness and ability."

The *Commercial* said, April 12th: "One of the ablest and most popular men on the State Bench. * 'His retirement is a public loss.'"

The *Enquirer*, April 12th: "Able, fair, and universally respected. His loss will be deeply felt and deplored."

Law Bulletin: "Industrious, pains-taking, conscientious, . . . working out with care and good discernment all the questions submitted to his judgment."

Penny Post: "An able, conscientious, upright judge.

Times-Star: "Very sincerely and generally regretted."

Volksfreund: "Regretted by judges, lawyers, and the whole public. . ."

FORAKER'S BRIEFS.

Foraker's briefs as a lawyer are remarkable for seizing the salient points and presenting his case with no superfluous verbiage. His decisions as a judge are eminently perspicuous, composed in pure English, conforming to the use which is natural and reputable and present, and manifesting a remarkable disposition to state the whole case, using the methods of logic leading to the conclusion. A learned jurist remarked that for a judge of his few years in life and at the bar, his decisions and their presentation are unexcelled, and are indeed models of their kind; that he is " able to see the point in a case and to state the conclusions in a clear and concise manner. He is a sound, forcible reasoner, and has good judgment. He has never debased himself or degraded his friends in seeking office."

His charge to the jury in a case of popular interest has been quoted as a remarkable example of legal and evidential analysis. Its conclusion illustrates the character of the man, in whom the public is now much interested:

" I need not say that you have nothing to do with consequences. I will not call your attention to the fact that you are not to consider the person of the plaintiff, nor of defendant. Courts and juries can accomplish tho purposes of their creation by only conscientiously doing their duty, without regard to parties or results." Thus spoke the incorruptible judge, uninfluenced by wealth of the parties or by popular considerations.

ALWAYS A REPUBLICAN.

Foraker was a Republican youth and his first vote was cast for Republican candidates.

Senator Sherman says Judge Foraker has carried the Republican banner in war and in peace, without halting by the wayside.

Judge Foraker did not regard the Republican party as an association to obtain the spoils of office, but as born of the conscience of the people ; its motive, justice ; its purpose, to restore the government to it original lines, moving forward with the boldness of earnest conviction, denouncing slavery as an outrage and a crime, assailing the doctrine that capital should own labor, seeing in the constitution abundant power to repress slavery, promote education, foster industry, encourage internal improvement, establish free homesteads and promote free discussion. He did not regard the victory of 1860 as a transfer of power from the Democratic to the Republican party, but as the beginning of a new life, which conquered the great rebellion, raised an army, constructed a navy, maintained the public credit, destroyed slavery, and provided for development. He says our wonderful prosperity has not come by chance, but is the effect of the political logic of the Republican party of 1860.

NO SPOILS OF OFFICE.

Judge Foraker could not consistently vote with the Democratic party, as he did not seek the spoils of office. He could not vote with the Democratic party, because of its views of the States and the Constitution ; because the Democratic party asserted state sovereignty at the command of the slave power ; because the Democratic party brought on the war of secession; because the Democratic party (though many individual Democrats were patriotic) opposed the subduing of the rebellion and enforcing the unity of the Republic ; and because Democratic organizations resisted the

4

measures of the Government. He could not join the Democratic party because its last administration of affairs brought the government to the verge of bankruptcy, had defied the constitution in eleven states, and arrayed an army against the nation; because the party had never apologized for its errors nor retracted its opinions; because this party was the enemy of free elections and of a pure ballot, the enemy of American industry. He realized that the patriotic element of the Democratic party had largely come into the Republican party, and that the Democratic party had become an artifice for office — controlled and manipulated by office-hunters; that the Democratic party had ceased to exist, in the sense of a body of citizens formed around a political question to effect a political object by united action to that political end, and that the last act of the party organized to uphold and enlarge the area of slavery, was to organize a rebellion of slave provinces in support of its political idea, and that the Democratic party was without reason of existence after the rebellion was crushed and now it exists by force of habit, inherited prejudice, or appetite for office.

FREEDOM AND CIVIL RIGHTS.

Supporting the war as a soldier, in times of peace he favored reconstruction measures to secure the fruits of victory and to establish the freedom and civil rights of the late slaves. In 1874, Judge Foraker, at a Republican mass meeting at Cincinnati, on the civil rights question, said:

" The object of this bill is to prevent masked marauders from burning negro school-houses, shooting negro school teachers, and keeping this innocent and inoffensive people in a state of terror, which retards their development and corrupts and demoralizes society and politics in a hundred ways. And it is right, and the Republican party is for it because it is right.

" When in Columbus the other day, I stood in our capitol building and looked with admiring gaze upon that magnificent painting, which adorns its walls, of " Perry's Victory on the Lake." There, in the midst of the death-storm of that terrible conflict, as gallant looking as any one of the brave faces surrounding the Commodore, is a full-blooded representative of the African race. And thus it has always been since our government was founded, on land and on sea, in adversity and prosperity, through peace and through war, this race has been ever present with us, and never once has its faith faltered, its devotion lagged, or its courage failed.

" They have justly earned their citizenship, and they have earned it in such a way as that for us not to protect them in it would be the basest ingratitude and wrong—ingratitude and wrong for which the nation would deserve to sink to rise no more."

* ❊ ❊ ❊ ❊ ❊ ❊ ❊ ❊

JUDGE FORAKER'S NOMINATION

Judge Foraker's nomination for governor was spontaneous in southern Ohio, and soon became popular throughout the State as candidates were canvassed. It was not sought for by Foraker. No efforts were made to secure the nomination. No whiskey nor unworthy devices, and no money were employed to affect votes. No certificates was furnished that he "satisfied his appetite for spirituous liquors," and that he was "neither a temperance man nor a Sunday fanatic."

When it came to the serious determination of the large and able convention gathered from all over the State, there was but one voice and but one unanimous acclamation for the farmer and soldier boy of Rocky Creek.

NOBLE TESTIMONY.

The following extracts from an interesting correspondence between the colored people and Judge Foraker, shows the grateful regard of the former and the noble sentiments of the Judge, who places suffrage upon pure manhood, and who bears his testimony for the Christian religion and for a pure domestic life.

The Judge regards the building up of families as the epitomized history of the American people for more than two hundred years —the central idea at Jamestown, at Plymouth Rock, at Charlestown, at Philadelphia, at Baltimore ; by the Puritans, by the Cavaliers, by the Quakers, and by the Roman Catholics ; the family, the social, and the political unit of America.

The colored people invited the Judge to a camp-meeting. They said, (June 19, 1883):

* * * ❊ * ❊ ❊ ❊

" We are religious people of color, and are Methodists. We remember those who have labored for our cause in the political field and on the field of battle. Joshua Giddings was not a Methodist, yet he was an Ohio champion of our cause. Salmon P. Chase was an Episcopalian, yet he never wavered in his devotion to the cause of our emancipation and elevation. We shall never forget the late Speaker of the House and our Republican Representatives, who carried on the memorable struggle for a fair count and a free ballot, and which seated our brethren, Smalls and Lynch. We are not ignorant as to your history and your early devotion on the battle field to the cause of our race. We have read your speeches and we trust you.

We know your mother to be a plain, old-fashioned Methodist, and we believe you to revere her religious principles.

Now can you not come up and give us an address of advice and encouragement?

*   *   *   *   *   *   *   *   *

To this the Judge replied :

CINCINNATI, June 23, 1883.

REV. AND DEAR SIRS:—Your kind letter of June 19, I find before me upon my return to the city. Make my apology to your associates for my seeming neglect.

It is now so very late in the week, and my previous engagements for this day and to-morrow are of such a character, that it is impossible for me to accept the invitation so kindly extended. Please return my thanks to your associates and the laity assembled, and express to them my appreciation, not only of their courtesy, but, also, of the good work in which they are engaged.

If our colored brethren will but continue in the future to cultivate religion and morality as they have in their free past, the day is not far distant when they will have conquered all prejudices that may have arisen, because of their being changed from serfs to citizens.

Religion and well-ordered domestic life, are the foundation of good and stable government. Without them the blessings of liberty and prosperity may be lost to us in anarchy and despotism.

The purity of the ballot box must be preserved. The franchise bestowed upon the men of your race because of their manhood, and not because of their color, must be enjoyed by you without fear or menace all over our land.   With sentiments of regard, I am

Yours truly, J. B. FORAKER.

Robert Harlan wrote June 15, 1883 :

"I know of my own personal knowledge that he has always been an earnest friend and supporter of my race in its struggle for its rights.

I remember well to have heard him make a speech to a mass meeting at Lower Market in this city, in 1874, when the civil rights bill was pending, in which he took a strong ground in favor of it, saying it was right, and that the Republican party could not hesitate about making it a law."

This is a portion of the speech of Judge Foraker alluded to by Mr. Harlan :

CIVIL RIGHTS BILL.

Another question about which the Democratic soul is troubled, is the Civil Rights Bill. This is not to be wondered at, however, for the poor, innocent colored man has always been a "bugaboo" to the Democracy. They have always been the enemy to this unfortunate race, and I suppose we can always count upon their opposition in advance to any proposition looking to the improvement of their condition.

The Civil Rights Bill does not confer upon the colored man a single legal right which he does not already possess.

For every colored man in this country has already the full legal right to sleep and eat in any hotel in the land, ride upon any common carriage, attend any public school, in short, do and enjoy any and all things that any other American citizen as such, can enjoy. Here in the North he enjoys these rights. The Civil Rights Bill does not therefore affect us here. But throughout the south the colored man is still called a "niggah," and he is not only denied these rights, but he is unceremoniously and unhumanly murdered and outraged if he dares to insist upon them. . . .

The negroes have been made free and have been made citizens, and clothed with all the rights and powers that pertain to the American citizens. It is unnecessary to rehearse the process and causes whereby this result has been reached. Sufficient it is to say that even the Democracy, in order to secure any favor whatever before the people, have been compelled to recognize the propriety and justness of this action, so earnest are the people in their approbation of it. And even the Democracy have been compelled to pledge themselves to maintain this condition of things, and take no step backward. If it was right then, as the whole country says it was, to make a citizen out of a negro, it is not only right now, but the duty of the government to secure him in the enjoyment of all that the title carries with it.

Young Men's Candidate.

Judge Foraker, as the young men's candidate, is a bright example to young men of the fruits of an honest, industrious, studious, temperate, patriotic, filial, and even religious life ; that there is something that gives success earlier than strong liquors, money, and demagoguism. Our first voters, our young men, will judge of Foraker by his life and his acts as they will judge of the party of which he is now the accepted leader in Ohio. Judge Foraker with his party fought for and maintained the integrity of the Union against secession and state-rights. He with the Republican party declared slavery a curse ; was with it for the freedom of all men and in clothing more than four million slaves in the garb of liberty and the full rights of citizen manhood. He was on the battle-field, when the party now opposing him declared the war a failure and was demanding an ignoble peace. He fought against tuc party that would have purchased peace at any price, at the expense of justice and the freedom of the slaves. He represents a party that turned out the rascals twenty years ago—turned out those who stole the money in the treasury; the rascals who rifled the arsenals, and who attempted to annihilate the Union. He is to day opposed to turning in the rascals who have caused the distress of our war, taxation, and the life sorrow of our households by the loss of father and brother and son.

IS HE UNKNOWN?

It will thus be seen that Judge Foraker is not an unknown man and is not without an enviable record; that he is known to the soldiers for his gallant bravery; that he is known as a lawyer at one of the strongest bars in the United States; that he is known as an able and careful jurist; that he is known to the colored people for his bold and strong advocacy of their rights; that he is known as the friend of the mechanic and of the laborer and of the farmer ; that he is known among the students and graduates of colleges; that he is known where sweet domestic life is valued; that he is known as a man of Christian integrity and of Christian principle; that he is known as the incorruptible politician, who seeks no office and wins no distinction by vile methods and the improper use of money; that he is known in his own county, in the chief city of Ohio, throughout the state, and is becoming known all over this land, not as a rich man and not as a mere politician ; and that he is unknown as Lincoln was, as Grant was, as Hays was,—and to be known as the next Governor of Ohio!

A Georgia paper candidly admits that Judge Foraker "has proved that he has in him the stuff of which governors are made. He is not afraid of the people. He appeals like a man to their reason and conscience, and discusses public affairs with the power of a master in reasoning and debate.

Senator Sherman thus spoke :

" Judge Foraker, the nominee of the Republican party, is a Republican soldier, who, as such, served his country when he was young. He has since been educated by his own efforts, and has attained an honorable distinction as a lawyer and a judge. His speeches are clear, bold, and manly, and express without evasion the principles of the Republican party—in favor of the protection of American labor, and in favor of the taxing the traffic in liquor and beer. In his speeches there is nothing evasive or uncertain."

Hon. Mr. Townsend, thus:

"Foraker, by his clear, practical, plain, common sense reasoning, is taking wonderful hold of the people. He is a fine stump-speaker. He never utters what can embarrass him or the cause of truth."

Gen. Gibson, thus:

"I regard him as one of the most successful campaign orators Ohio has ever produced. He speaks with ease and grace, his words are well chosen, sincere and impressive, and have an effective influence upon his audience. He comes before the public unpreceeded by a great reputation, and his hearers are astonished that they never knew him before. His character is perfect, his record clear, and his ability large. He is the cleanest and best man for Governor the State has known for thirty years, and, possibly, excepting John Brough, the ablest stumper. I told Hoadly when he was at my house in Tiffin, a short time ago, that he would suffer defeat if he allowed himself to go before the people in a joint discussion with Foraker.

Hon. General Noyes, late minister to France, said to the people of the Scioto Valley, in mass meeting assembled:

"The Republican party on the other hand, proud of its past and confident of its future, has consistently placed in nomination a man who was born a Republican, and who has remained one all his life; a Union soldier who has fought for his country, with a gun to his shoulder and a knapsack on his back; one who did not seek the nomination for Governor, but whom the office sought; a brilliant lawyer, an able debater, an upright, patriotic gentleman. Having called him away from a successful practice of his profession, we propose to elect him. What the future have in store we can not tell, but we may be sure Judge Foraker will deserve whatever honor may be in reserve for him."

THE PEOPLE IN EARNEST.

As we go to press, these are specimen reports from the meetings Judge Foraker is addressing:

LANCASTER, O., Sept. 3.

"Judge Foraker addressed one of the finest and largest mass meetings here this afternoon that has been held in this city for years. Everybody was surprised at the great crowd, which exceeded any meeting held during the last Presidential campaign. The City Hall was packed to its utmost capacity, hundreds being turned away for want of room. The Judge's speech was another of his masterly arraignments of the Democratic party, and held the vast audience enrapt until its close. He explained at length and to their satisfaction on the wool issue, showing just what it was, and what the opposition were trying to make of it. He also showed by his matchless argument just how impossible it was for Democratic success this fall, and how the Republicans are steadily marching on to a grand victory.

One old Democrat who was an attentive listener to the Judge's address, said he did not wonder that Hoadly was sick; his only surprise was that he was alive at all.

He told what he had seen and heard among both Republicams and Democrats throughout the State, and gave the people a clear understanding of the true status of affairs. Foraker's facts and figures consummately upset the Democratic wool bugaboo, and clearly demonstrated what a ludicrous farce the whole thing is. It was a splendid speech, and has left a telling effect."

From Zanesville, Sept. 4 :

"Judge Foraker addressed the greatest hall meeting ever held in this city. Never before in local annals have voters manifested so great a willingness to endure the discomforts of a crowd."

We now supplement the foregoing by extracts .rom addresses of Judge Foraker, further illustrating the man and his principles.

The following was delivered at a Banquet at the Burnett House, given to the Loyal Legion of Philadelphia, Pa., February 3, 1883, in response to the toast:

"OHIO."

MR. COMMANDER AND FELLOW-COMPANIONS:

No matter what the occasion may be, it is always a great pleasure to an Ohio man to talk about Ohio. Particularly is this true of what may be termed these war occasions, such as this to-night. For great as our state is considered to be in area, business, population, art, and education, in all that pertains to the civilization and improvement of mankind, she is transcendantly greater still in all that relates to the part taken by her in the great struggle. From the firing of the first gun on Fort Sumpter until the surrender of Lee at Appomattox, she was continually at the very fore front, side by side with Pennsylvania, and the best and bravest of her sister states. Her sons displayed their valor, poured out their blood, and laid down their lives on every battle-field of the war. And I need not repeat in this presence that she contributed to our cause in that contest vastly more than her two hundred regiments of gallant fighting men. There are some names that have become as familiar as household words, the world over, in which she claims an especial interest—names around which cluster all the dazzling glories of triumphant war,—names, also, at the mere mention of which is suggested all that is implied by the highest, purest, and most successful accomplishments of enlightened statesmanship. For while Pennsylvania was giving us Mead and Hancock and brave John Reynolds, Ohio was giving to the country, and to the cause of humanity, not only Grant and Sheridan, Sherman and McPherson, but Chase and Wade and Stanton, also. And these illustrious names I have mentioned barely begin the long list of her scarcely less distinguished soldiers and statesmen who in that great trial won imperishable renown in field and cabinet.

OHIO EVER DISTINGUISHED.

As proof conclusive that our success then was based on merit, that the war was merely an exceptional opportunity, we have been no less distinguished since. This is shown by smaller as well as by greater things.

When a year or two ago the Messrs. Scribners undertook the issue of campaign histories of the war, to be written by different persons, in twelve volumes, and cast about to see who from the thirty-eight states of the Union should be selected as the most fit for the important work, the result was that four of the twelve volumes were allotted to Ohio.

"Continually since the war, of our Supreme Court, the highest, judicial tribunal in the land, consisting of nine members, we have had two of the number, and one of them the Chief Justice. And during all this while we have had both the General and the Lieutenant-General of the Army; and during almost all this time we have held at least a fair share of the most important heads of departments, and of the most important posts of representation abroad.

And, notwithstanding this every excess of favor, we have been twice called upon, without the place being sought in either instance, to furnish a chief magistrate for the whole people; and twice we have responded,—with what eminent success you all do know.

GARFIELD AND HAYES.

"So long as the history of the American people shall be read and known among men, so long in the tenderest recesses of the heart will be held in grateful recollection and proud esteem the name of James A. Garfield.

"It would not be in good taste to speak in the presence of our other ex-president the warm words of praise with which all would be pleased to hear to his many virtues recounted. Suffice it to say, he regards it as one of the highest honors of his distinguished life to be present with us to-night as simply *companion* Rutherford B. Hayes.

"I think I can truthfully say for Ohio that her past, at least, is secure; and I know whereof I affirm when I say that we have confidence in the present, and hope for the future. We may not be called upon to furnish any more presidents, generals, chief justices, secretaries, or foreigh ministers; but if so, that will be *your* fault and not *ours*. For I assure you we will not be discouraged thereby from keeping constantly on hand, and well advertised, an inexhaustible supply of the very best material. [Laughter.]

"I sincerely hope that these remarks will not excite apprehension in the minds of any of our visiting companions; for I am sure this Ohio acquisition has not as yet any designs upon the honors of this organization. On the contrary, I am quite positive that none of us expect offices right away. We expect to be required; and we shall be content with that—to patiently wait for all such matters until at least a reasonable probation shall have expired. I warn you though that we are a progressive class. We claim to be representative of our state; and being such, it is only fair to assume that when the expiration of this probation shall have come we will desire to be useful. From all I was able to learn from the speech of General Owen of the principles and purposes of this order, it is my judgment that it affords a first-class chance for the display of the talents of the average Ohio man. With its espousal of principles and its proclamation of purposes I know him to be entirely familiar. They have been his meat and drink all his life long. In fact, ever since good old Frances Dane wrote it down in his first organic law—the ordinance of 1787—for the government of the territory lying north-west of the river Ohio, that 'religion, morality, and knowledge were necessary to good government;' and that 'civil and religious liberty lay at the basis of all our constitutions and laws,' our Ohio man has had for his polar star what the charter of this order declares its principles to be. First, a firm belief and trust in Almighty God, under whose beneficence and guidance the triumphs of the war were achieved; and second,—and only second,—true allegiance to the United States of America, founded on fidelity and devotion to the constitution and laws of our government. [Loud applause and laughter.]

"With such antecedents as I have referred to, such an education as I have described, and such aspirations as all concede us, I confidently predict that the future will afford us a chance, both in this order and outside of it, commensurate with the glorious grandeur of the past; and that as the years go gliding by, the name of Ohio, linked with and second only to that of Pennsylvania, shall continue, like that of Ben Adhem, to lead all the rest." [Prolonged applause.]

THE BOYS IN BLUE.

A prophet is sometimes honored in his own home. Judge Foraker was so by the " Boys in Blue," at the soldier's reunion and fourth of July celebration of this year (1883), within the borders of his native county. Old veterans and their wives, not away from their neighborhood since the war, went twenty miles to see this Highland private, this hero of Atlanta.

How like a true man, with domestic and popular sympathies, how like Lincoln breaking forth, " why should the spirit of mortals be proud," was Foraker in his speech of this day among the neighbors, the friends, the men once boys on Rocky Creek. He spoke without notes, from a full heart. He spoke as Lincoln, and Garfield spoke, men poor in this world's wealth, but rich in the treasures of a noble heart. He said :

" Here I regard myself as in an especial sense in my own country; for here I am within the borders of Highland County, and when I come within the boundary lines of this county, I feel as though I had come within the walls of my own home, and on this account I can say, in response to the kind words of your chairman, that if there is any place on the face of the earth where I would rather enjoy the confidence and esteem of mankind than another, it is here ; in this county where, as he has said, I was born and reared, and where for that reason I am better known than I can ever hope to become at any other place, and where I have friends that I know will always remain such without regard to any difference of opinion that may exist as to temporal concerns, and without regard to the varying fortunes and changes of life. For me to come into your midst is like gliding into a veritable haven of rest where all the frictions and buffetting contentions of an anxious and busy life, are for the time being, shut out by a general amity of feeling, and by sentiments of a kind and mutual regard.

.   .   .   .

" We are here to-day not only to celebrate the Fourth of July, but we have come here to perform this work in the name, in the honor, and under the direction of the Grand Army of the Republic.

" We are here, therefore, not only to pay honor to the initial work of the founders of these institutions of government, in the enjoyment of which it is our happy privilege to live, but also to pay honor to the men by whose services and sacrifices, patriotism and valor, these institutions of government have been preserved to us from the threatened wreck and ruin of rebellion. But for the works of the fathers, there never would have been any occasion for the services of the sons, and but for the services of the sons, that which the fathers did would have been done in vain. . . . .

"One hundred years of successful experience under a republican form of government, has taught us not only to regard the ideas and truths and principles embodied in the Declaration of Independence, as fundamental proposition with respect to the character of government and the rights of man, but it has also brought us to the point where it is well nigh impossible for us to realize that there ever was a time in the history of the world when they were not so regarded. . . . . .

MAGNA CHARTA AND LUTHER.

"And yet, notwithstanding our fathers were lacking in these respects, notwithstanding they were without precedent, and without anything in the way of experience to guide them, they were not without the essentials of success. On the contrary, they had that without which there could have been no success, but with which success was inevitable, for they had that which nerved the hearts of the old Lords and Barons when they wrestled Magna Charta from King John, at Runnymede; they had that which filled the soul of brave old Luther, when he said : 'Yes sir, I will go into that city of Worms, though there be as many devils there as there are tiles on the roofs of the houses.'

" They had just convictions of right, and they had the courage of their convictions, and that was the key to the whole situation.

"For when men have a just and proper sense of duty, and then fearlessly undertake its performance, Providence never fails to lead them safely through, whatever consequences may result." . . . .

MEN MUST BE RIGHT.

That which they accomplished makes the most striking and brilliant illustration that has ever been given of the truth to which I adverted a moment ago, that all political movements must succeed when they are based on just convictions of right, and are fearlessly and boldly espoused and upheld. Their works makes a fitting frontispiece for the grand career that this Nation has run. It was a work that never has and never will fail to impart Inspiration and honesty of purpose to political organizations when called upon to grapple with those insiduous evils that affect the morality of the people, and snap at the foundations of government. It was an example that exerted a most salutory influence on us while we were passing through the great struggles with slavery. It is a good example to bear in mind in connection with the contests now going on in this country, and no matter what may be the growth and complications of the future, we can always turn to this beginning of the fathers, with pleasure, pride and profit.

After describing the grandeur of our country, its present population, and its vast capabilities, the Judge continued :

But I do not make these suggestions for the purpose of exciting vanity. On the contrary, I make them to bring about a properly serious appreciation of the great trust that is confided in us—a trust that involves for all these millions of people and billions of property the preservation of our form of government, our constitution, our civil and religious liberty, our popular education, our equality before the law—a preservation, in short, of all that which makes us free, and makes us great, and makes us safe in the protection of our property and our lives.

In replying to the proposition that our institutions are not adapted to the conditions of the future, he said :

And remembering, as all must who passed through the trials of 1861-5, how this whole land was made to fairly blaze and burn by the unparalleled demonstrations of loyalty, patriotism and devotion to duty which we then witnessed, I can not doubt either the capacity or the determination of the people of this country to preserve its government and its institutions

PRACTICAL PATRIOTISM.

And yet, to do so, we must be for the future as we have been in the past, true to ourselves. I believe in a practical patriotism. I believe in taking care of America. To this end we should discard sentimental theories and pursue an administrative policy that is based on sound common sense. We should make this country independent of every other to the fullest extent that our situation and advantages will admit. We must take care of our labor and laboring men, to the end that they may have a just reward and an even chance in the race of life for those better and higher things that come with education and culture. We must develop our resources, multiply our industries, and make as much diversity of employment as possible, thus creating a domestic commerce that will make all the different parts of our country virtually dependent on each other, and lead on to the construction of railroads and canals, and other facilities for traffic and travel, thus tying ourselves together with the bonds of trade and interest which are far stronger and more enduring than any that can be forged by constitutional provision or legistative enactments.

WASHINGTON AND DANE.

And not only that, but man can not live by bread alone. Our fathers recognized this fact when they framed our government. They, therefore, framed it so as to encourage not only the greatest material prosperity possible, but also so as to encourage the highest intellectual and moral development of which mankind is capable. Washington reminds us of this in his farewell address, when he warns us to remember that the people are the sovereign power—that all rightful authority must emanate from them, and that, consequently, if we would have a good government, we must have a good people, and that to that end we must ever labor to inculcate among the people a disposition for knowledge and morality. Another of the greatest men that this country ever produced was Francis Dane. He was the author of "the ordinance of 1788 for the government of the territory lying nothwest of the River Ohio." This was the first organic law that the people of Ohio ever had. In it is expressed the idea to which I refer in the declaration that knowledge and morality are essential to good government. All the founders and all the great men of this government, from Washington to Garfield, have impressed upon us the same truth.

And above all things let us remember to preserve and inviolate the dignity and majesty of law. As Washington said, we have no sovereignty in this country except only the people. Law is their expressed will, and the officers of the law are only their agents. Whosoever undertakes to strike down law in this country, either by open violence or by exciting distrust, is aiming a deadly blow at the very life of the Nation.

GRAND ARMY—A FIRST BOOK.

Thus spoke this soldier to his comrades of the Grand Army of Republic in his own native county, July 4, 1383:

"I remember that one of the first books my father ever gave me was a history of the Revolution, bound in which was a *fac simile* copy of the Declaration of Independence, including the signatures thereto of all the signers. I can never forget how, in my boyish ambition, I envied those men the honor of having signed that instrument. I have no doubt you had the same kind of experience. But you didn't know then of the compensation that was in store for you. Your names can never be read on the Declaration of Independence, but they will be read so long as that declaration is remembered on the muster rolls of that grand army of a million men that sprang to the Nations rescue and stood like a wall of fire between the country and the country's danger. And to have your names written there is the highest honor that your country's service has permitted you to achieve in your day and generation. As I said a while ago, but for your services all that the fathers did would have been done in vain. The men who inaugurated the rebellion put themselves beyond the pain of reason at the outset. They wouldn't listen to argument. All the logic and all the eloquence of Webster, although absolutely unanswerable, were nevertheless unavailing. They wouldn't be convinced, and couldn't be persuaded. They had made up their minds that if they couldn't rule this Union they would break it up and destroy it. They invented their doctrine of State sovereignty for that purpose, and when, in their judgment, the time was ripe for it they invoked it, and involved this whole country in war to sustain it. But that which argument could not settle, shot and shell did. On three hundred bloody battle-fields, and in the blood of three hundred thousand of our slain fathers and brothers and sons it was written with the bayonet amid the storm-clouds of war that this is a Nation. Webster was vindicated and the Union was preserved. The character of our Constitution was taken out of all controvesy, and there was established for it, as one of its elementary features, that it was just what on its face it expressed itself to be, not a league between States, but the organic law a great people, and as to the rights and powers by it delegated supreme over States and people alike. There were many good results of that war, but this was the richest prize we brought out of all that bloody struggle. Let us hold on to it. Let us keep it to the fore-front.

1798.

Divide as we may about other matters, let us ever remember to stand shoulder to shoulder for this. When you hear a man talking about the reserved rights of the States and the resolutions of 1798, as we occasionally do, set him down as a man that no soldier can afford to listen to. So much we owe to the brave comrades we left behind when we marched home in victorious triumph. We owe so much to ourselves, and we especially owe it to our country and our posterity. Not that we would keep alive any of the animosities or prejudices of the war, but simply that we would have no foolishness about the preservation of what we won. We were in serious earnest then. There has been too much blood shed to permit of our becoming otherwise now.

No soldier wishes to keep alive any animosities or prejudices. On the contrary, it is our earnest hope that they may all perish with the hated doctrine of secession that originated them. We fought the South and compelled them to stay in the Union, not because we hated and despised them, but because they belonged to us, because they were part and parcel of us, because their country was our country, and their destiny was our destiny. We compelled them to stay in the Union, not that we might live together in jarring discord, but that we might have a perpetual peace and a common prosperity.

THE SECESSIONIST—THE REGICIDE.

We can rejoice to-day in the fact that the chasms of the war are being rapidly bridged over. You couldn't to-day give slavery back to the South as a free and gracious gift. They appreciate as keenly as anybody else can that the abolition of it was a great blessing for them. Their country is now everywhere prospering as it never did before, and the day is not far distant when the secessionist of 1861 will be known in this country only as the regicide is known in England. We will have a Union in fact as well as in name, and every section will vie with every other in a common devotion to a common flag, by which we will all be led in a common prosperity to a common destiny.

THE GALLANT UNKNOWN.

From the decoration-day address of 1869, at Hillsboro, which was delivered, says the *Highland News*, "with deep and earnest feeling, with grace and dignity, impressing all with the great ability of the young orator : "

" There are many graves in this land to-day, equally as deserving as the ones we have honored, about which no kind tribute-payers are gathered. Not all the bodies that fell by the ravages of our war sleep in our cemeteries.

"Far away in the woods, the thicket, the mountain gaps; on the barren plain, the deserted field, in a hundred kinds of hidden, obscure, and unfrequented places, wherever, on the hard-fought field, the deathful missil of the enemy reached and struck them down, lie and sleep another band— *the gallant unknown.*

"God, in his infinite wisdom and goodness, as though jealously reserving it unto himself, has thus deprived us of the pleasurable privilege of decorating their graves. But while he has done this, there is another pleasurable privilege and pleasurable duty, of which he has not deprived us, and that is of constantly remembering them, and praying him that he may annually stretch forth his hand and causing to descend "the earlier and the latter rains," make to grow thereon flowers even more luxuriant, more fragrant, and more enduring, than the ones which to-day have been scattered by the fair hands of these beautiful little girls upon the graves of our known ; scattering there, I shall add, only that they may fade and whither, and perish, and pass away, typifying, as it were, the untimely snapping, and perishing, and passing away of the lives of those whom they are intended to honor."

CHEAP TRANSPORTATION.

From Judge Foraker's address at Cincinnati :

Although the question of cheap transportation is of vast importance, I can say but a word :

The Constitution of the United States confers upon Congress the power to regulate commerce among the states. No restrictions are placed upon its exercise. We contend that the provision was framed in the way, intentionally, that it might be broad enough to cover all times and circumstances. And hence, notwithstanding the fact that railroads were not known when the Constitution was framed, yet, inasmuch as they have become a chief means of commerce among the states, they are within the purview of the provision, as well as rivers, lakes and harbors.

Fortunately, before it ever entered into politics, this question was, quite a number of times, raised and passed upon by the courts, and in every such instance the provision was construed as we contend it should be. So far then as the right to exercise the power is concerned, it is no longer an open question, The democracy, true to their natural instincts, have doggedly arrayed themselves on the wrong side, and are amusing themselves with their ancient political Shibboleth, "unconstitutional."

The propriety of exercising this power is a question to be determined by the particular facts of a given case.

But when the facts are that millions of bushels of grain are raised in this country which never get to a market, and consequently never result in any profit to the producer, simply because the lines of railway passing through the different states lying between the markets and the points of production, charge unreasonably large freights, I think Congress should look after the matter and correct the evil, if there be any remedy, because so long as such a condition of things exists, agriculture is discouraged throughout vast territories of our country, and all kinds of improvement and progress are delayed and hindered.

This is the position af the Republican party, and it is the right position, for it is upon the side of the correct construction and a proper enforcement of a good law, framed by the wise fathers who made our constitution, to protect the people and aid the prosperity of the Government.

The financial platform of the Republican party to-day, as in the past, is nothing more nor less than a pledge that we will continue in the future as we have done in the past to retrench and economize, and cut down the expenses of the Government to the lowest possible sum consistent with a wise and intelligent policy. That we will lighten the burdens of taxation resting upon the people just as rapidly, and just as much as proper regard for the highest interests of all will allow. That we will continue to faithfully and diligently collect the revenues, and honestly and promptly apply them to the satisfaction and diminution of the public debt, until, in this honest, straight forward, practical, common-sense way we have, by easy and natural stages, and without shock, precipitation or derangement, led the country back, as we have been leading it, to the solid basis of specie payments, and then on to an entire discharge of this enormous indebtedness.

We propose to pay the debt simply by paying it, and by paying it dollar for dollar until every obligation of the Government has been fully redressed, to the last farthing.

To this end we propose neither expansion nor contraction, but the application of every surplus dollar we may be able to get into the treasury to the payment of interest bearing bonds held by private individuals in whose hands they are non-taxable, and yield no support whatever.

NO PATIENCE WITH TREASON.

At Spring Grove and Wesleyan cemeteries, Cincinnati, May 31, 1879, Judge Foraker said :

" If any man think there is less patriotism in the country, less devotion to the Union, less love and affection for the old flag—let him look abroad over the land on this National Decoration Day and be undeceived. Let him witness the impressive spectacle of a whole people gathered in sorrow, but with the choicest flowers of spring time in their hands about the graves of their dead soldiers. Let him listen to the patriotic hymns that will be sung, the fervid sentiments of patriotism that will be expressed, and from these things let him learn that the loyalty of this people is as unquestioned as ever. Yea, let him learn more than that ! Let him learn, especially if he be a Confederate Brigadier in Congress demanding that every vestige of war legislation be torn from the statute book, or a so-called "silver tongued orator" from the Blue Grass regions talking about the rebel dead being martyrs to a holy cause that is to be revived and vindicated in the near future, let him I say, especially, if he be one of these classes, learn that by so much as we mourn these lives by so much is there less of patience for treason than ever before.

    *   *   *   *   *   *   *

Abraham Lincoln was elected President of the United States. There was no pretense that any section of the country, or any individual even, would be interfered with in the enjoyment of any right or privilege guaranteed under the Constitution and the laws of the land. But that did not matter ; the galling fact still remained that the control of the government had passed out of the hands of the South. The North had gained ascendancy in national affairs, and was likely to maintain it, and that was enough. The chivalric sons of the South wouldn't submit to any such outrage as that. The time against which the conspirators had plotted was come. A practical application of the doctrine they had taught was now in order.

SHORT WORK WITH TRAITORS.

And, consequently, in braggart speeches, for which the authors ought to have been then and there arrested and hanged by the neck until dead, we were told that the Union of the fathers was dissolved, that the Constitution was torn into shreds and tatters, that the South had seceded, and that all they asked of us was that we would quietly remain at home and behave ourselves while they went their way in peace. Not until these initial proceedings in the great drama of secession were actually transpiring, did our people awaken to anything like a proper appreciation of the infamous character of the doctrine that had been invoked. But then it was, as in bewildered amazement and astonishment they found themselves confronted with the necessity of a choice between the calamities of a civil war or a dissolution of the Union, that the fires of patriotism began to burn in their bosoms—fires of patriotism that found fitting expression at the lips of that gallant old patriot when he commanded, "If any man attempt to haul down the American flag, shoot him on the spot." Fires of patriotism that were shortly to blaze into a flame that would astonish and excite the admiration of the whole world. For the same match that fired the first shot against old Fort Sumpter, and the stars and stripes waving over her, at the same time fired the patriotic hearts of the loyal millions of the North, and there followed the most magnificent demonstration of patriotism and devotion that the world ever witnessed. Business pursuits, private interests, family and social ties, the pleasures and comforts of home, attachments, endearments, affections—everything that stood in the way was instantly sacrificed by a million gallant heroes who sprang to the nation's rescue."

ONE COUNTRY—ONE FLAG.

At the Camp Fire, October 5, 1880, of Geo. H. Thomas' Post No. 13, G. A. R., the subject of Judge Foraker's address was "One Country and One Flag." After giving the history of the two civilizations, that from Plymouth Rock and that from Jamestown, the Judge proceeds:

BOYS IN BLUE.

"Jealousy ripened into hostility and hostility brought blood. 'One country and one flag' would no longer answer. Slavery demanded two countries and two flags. They claimed it as a legal and constitutional right. Webster met their claim, annihilated their arguments, and showed conclusively that they had no such right. . . . He appealed to the recollections of the past, when Massachusetts and South Carolina stood shoulder to shoulder acknowledging Independence. But they steeled their hearts and the dash of arms came. When the boom from the guns at Fort Sumter rolled up over our land its reverberating echoes filling our valleys and breaking against our mountain sides, it was as a long roll calling a nation to duty—a long roll that was answered by a million men; a million men who were not educated and professional soldiers; a million men to whom war was no opportunity to work out individual ambitions and aspirations; but a million volunteers—citizen soldiers—a million men to whom war was only a horrible and bloody evil to be resorted to only for the accomplishment of great purpose, and then only when nothing else would answer; a million men who were working out their individual ambitions and aspirations in the peaceful pursuits of civil life; a million men who had homes and families, and professions and farms and workshops to leave behind; men, therefore, who sacrificed all these things and stepped between their country and their country's danger with that solemn and determined resolve that only men can take who are actuated by a sense of responsible duty; a resolve that come what would—come separation from home, from wives, from children and loved ones; come exposures, come hardships, come sickness, come battle, come death, come whatsoever God in his providence might tend there should be in this country but one government and one flag, and that should be the government of the constitution and the flag that our fathers gave us.

"These were the 'Boys in Blue,' and when the boys in blue thus took up the discussion it meant there was to come an end of it; that we were to have no more unavailing arguments; that if word's wouldn't convince shot and shell should; and they did.

*　　*　　*　　*　　*　　*　　*

ONE NATION.

"If there be anything at all that soldiers cannot afford to listen to argument about; about which they cannot afford to admit that there is room for argument; anything which they are under obligation to at all times treat with impatient indignation, it is that damnable heresy that is eternally arraying the State against the Nation.

"If the war accomplished anything at all it was the overthrow of that idea, and the establishment upon its ruins of that other idea that the American people are an American Nation. A nation for Ohio or New York or

5

Massachusetts, nor yet for South Carolina or Alabama or Georgia—not a nation for the States at all, but a nation for the people and the whole people of all the States of the whole Union.

* * * * * * * * *

INFAMOUS IDEA.

I hope the day is not far distant when it shall be established that the general government may lawfully stretch forth its arm of protecting power to unprotected citizens at home as well as abroad. It is an infamous idea that the national government can not go into any State of the Union and compel any citizen to render its service against its enemies, and that when he shall have faithfully served it and been discharged, and shall have returned to his home, his State lines are to rise up so high about him that the government he has protected at the peril of his life cannot cross over them to his protection in the enjoyment of all the rights to which he is entitled under a Republican form of government.

"It is not enough so answer that it is the duty of the State to afford this protection.

"It is not enough, because by unpunished barbarities, horrible enough to shock and disgrace savages, we have been afforded most abundant as well as most painful evidence that the State may not do its duty. I hope the bloody outrages of Hamburg, Coushatta, and the murder of the Chisholms will never again be repeated to disgrace our land and civilization, but should the misfortune of their re-enactment be visited upon us, I earnestly trust there may be no counterpart to the great crime for which we, as citizens, must bear the responsibility, in a lack of power on the part of government somewhere to visit speedy and fitting justice upon the perpetrators.

"I want to see, therefore, not only one government and one flag for our whole country, but I want that government to be strong enough to go into every nook and corner of the whole land, not simply to collect its revenues, its taxes on whisky and tobacco, but what is infinitely more important and more to our credit, to protect the lives of its citizens and redress their wrongs and grievances. And I want the flag that is to stand for this government to symbolize all this to every man who looks with allegiance upon its folds. With such a country and such a flag there is nothing of patriotic reverence and affection that they will not enjoy. With such a country and such a flag, there is nothing of strength that will not be added unto us as a Nation. With such a country and such flag we can press forward into the future with a confident assurance that there is a destiny for us commensurate in grandeur and magnificence with the advantages we possess."

Of Judge Foraker's Decoration-day Address at Springfield, May 30, 1881, the Springfield *Republican* said:

"The mention of names of well-remembered commanders brought the applause of the audience every time; and frequently was this repeated at other periods of the grand effort of twenty-five minutes' duration. Attention was really strained at times. At affecting passages, particularly the references to mothers and wives of our dead soldiers, many eyes filled involuntarily. The address was in full keeping with the spirit of the hour, unambiguous, often impassioned, and delivered with impressiveness which had a marked effect. Although a comparative stranger in Springfield, the gentleman will be remembered with affection and admiration by all that vast audience. He unmistakably created a very favorable impression among the most intelligent class of people.

The Judge said :

" This imposing demonstration has a wide and an inspiring significance. It means more than that these men were brave. It means more than that they were our fathers and sons and husbands and brothers. It means more than that we loved them. It means more than that we owe them a debt we can never discharge for a nation preserved by the lives they surrendered. It means more than a tribute of honor and gratitude and affection for the dead. Its chief lesson is for the living.

SOLDIER'S SACRIFICES NOT FORGOTTEN.

" It means that the sacrifices of that time are not to be forgotten ; that they are to be kept in perpetual remembrance as the price paid for a nation purified and preserved ; kept in remembrance, however, not to keep alive any bitterness or hatred or prejudice that may have been engendered by that strife, but kept alive to cultivate and strengthen and cherish in our recollections that spirit of patriotism, loyalty, and devotion to duty that inspired our heroic dead.

" It means that these men died for the cause of all mankind, and that their lives and sacrificial deaths are worthy to be held in perpetual remembrance and continual honor as bright examples for the emulation of the living. It means that we do not propose to have to do that work over again. It means that here is the most sacred spot that can be found ; here in the most solemn presence that can be invoked ; here on these graves, as upon the altars of our country, we come to pledge ourselves anew to the preservation of that nationality and those eternal principles of truth and justice for which these men were slain. Then,

> " ' Cover them over with beautiful flowers,
> Deck them with garlands, these brothers of ours,
> Lying so silent by night and by day,
> Sleeping the years of their manhood away :
> Years they had marked for the joys of the brave,
> Years they must waste in the moldering grave.
> All the bright laurels they wasted to bloom,
> Fell from their hopes when they fell to the tomb.
> Give them the meed they have won in the past ;
> Give them the honors their futures forecast ;
> Give them the chaplets they won in the strife ;
> Give them the laurels they won with their life.
> Cover them over—yes, cover them over—
> Parent, husband, brother, and lover ;
> Crown in your hearts these dead heroes of ours,
> And cover them over with beautiful flowers.

It is a grand and inspiring work in which we are engaged. Let us be careful not to abuse its privileges or pervert its purposes. Let us not permit ourselves to be blinded or misled by that sickly and inconsistent spirit of sentimentality that has been here and there manifesting itself in a disposition to blot out all distinctions by scattering flowers alike over the Blue and they Gray.

NO BITTERNESS.

" Toward the dead soldiers of the South no heart can hold any bitterness, but it does not follow that we should pay them honor. We know they were brave ; we know they fought gallantly, and, for the sake of argument, we can afford to admit that they believed they were right. But all that does not and can not change the everlasting fact that they were not right, but wrong, and criminally and treasonably wrong, too. All that does not change the fact that they made this land to run red with rivers of blood, and filled our homes with widows and orphans, and weeping and morning, in a causeless and wicked endeavor to tear down and destroy the best government the wisdom of man ever devised, simply because its genius was Liberty, that they might establish for themselves, in its stead, another, based upon and inspired by human slavery. In their graves with them we can bury everything except, only, a vigilant watchfulness against a repetition of their treason; but to decorate their graves, at the same time and in the same way we decorate the graves of our fallen Union soldiers, would be to do an act that would be worse than a crime against the dead, and to teach a lesson that would be worse than meaningless to the living.

BOYS IN BLUE NOT TO BE DISHONORED.

"Whatever else we may do, may God save us from a criminal stupidity that would dishonor the boy in blue, who fought for the Union and the Constitution, the equality of all men before the law, and all the other great and grand ideas that underlie and vitalize our institutions, by holding him up to posterity as on an equality with the men who fought to uphold treason, destroy our nationality, and make shipwreck of all the bright hopes of self-government. Let us not do ourselves the injustice nor posterity the injury of indicating by such an act that we no longer know any difference between the men who saved us and the men who would have destroyed us.

GLORIOUS OLD MOTHERS.

On the contrary, when we are done decorating our Union dead, if we have any flowers to spare, instead of destroying all the good we have done by throwing them upon the Confederate dead, let us rather, in God's name, intensify the lesson we teach by lovingly scattering them over the glorious old mothers of the war; the glorious old mothers who followed us down into the smoke and fire of battle with fervent prayers to heaven for our preservation and for the success of our cause; the glorious old mothers who, with heroic words of patriotism, steeled the hearts and nerved the arms of the gallant boys with whom they now are sleeping; or over the tender and loving wives who, with hearts broken with grief, have prematurely followed down into the damp, cold grave the husbands they kissed farewell forever amid war's wild alarms; or let us weave them into bright chaplets with which to crown the children of our patriot dead—the children to whom the preservation of the nation meant orphanage and poverty and destitution; or in some other way let us do something that will be patriotic—something we can respect ourselves for —something that will redound to the honor of our dead, the credit of ourselves, and the good of our country.

Until the time shall come when all talk about the right and truth and justice of the "lost cause" shall be hushed forever—until equal and exact justice is freely accorded to every American citizen in every state in the Union—until the exercise of all the rights, privileges, and franchises of citizenship is as free and untrammeled wherever the flag floats as our slain heroes intended it to be, let us have a jealous care as to what we do, even with our flowers. Not, as I have already said, because of any feeling toward the dead, but for the effect upon the living. We must never forget that our Government is a Government of the people. It will be whatever the people make it, and they will make it whatever they are themselves; and what the people will be depends upon what they are taught.

Because of the teachings of our fathers the war found us ready to meet it. We have made the country free; we have made it a fundamental idea that the constitution is the organic law of the whole people; that the

General Government, as to the powers and functions delegated to it, is supreme from ocean to ocean, and that the American people are an American nation. These are grand results. They are worth all the blood and treasure they have cost. It was our highest duty to secure them then; it is our highest duty to preserve them now.

A PATRIOTIC IRISHMAN.

A patriotic Irishman, who had lost his mother while he was in the patriotic army, was so affected by the Springfield address in its allusion to decorating the graves of the mothers who had given their sons to the war, that he walked many miles to see and hear the man, at Leesburg, who had heart enough to make such a speech. He went away from the Leesburg address saying, "That's the man for me, with a head level enough to command an army, and a heart big enough to capture the soldiers."

THE UNITED STATES—OUR COUNTRY.

Judge Foraker made an address January 13, 1881, before the society of Ex-Army and Navy officers, whose names are a synonym of valorous deeds; the theme being "The United States—our Country." The Judge adverted to our vast domain; to our self-government; to our civil and religious liberty; to our thrift, ingenuity, enterprise and industry; to our illustrious past, the inspiring present and the grand future, and to our grave and increasing responsibilities : He concludes :

"Grave, therefore, as are the responsibilities that rest upon us, yet I confidently predict that they will be fully and faithfully discharged, and that as the years go by we shall not only continue to increase in numbers and grow in wealth, but that we shall see all sectional prejudices and animosities forgotten and swallowed up in a generous rivalry and a common pride; that we shall continue to be one people, maintaining one government, supporting the same Constitution, and following a common flag to a common destiny, thus verifying the prophetic assertion of the lamented Lincoln when he said, at Gettysburg, in those beautiful, impressive, and ever memorable words: "Government of the people, by the people and for the people, shall not perish from the earth."

LAW AND ORDER.

Judge Foraker presided Sunday night, 1882, at a meeting of citizens in the Methodist church, Walnut Hills, in the interest of law and order. In his address he said that the majesty and dignity of law must be preserved. * * He had an abiding faith in Providence and the common sense of the American people. * * Morality is the foundation of the Republic. and thus morality is dependent on religion.

THE LAST DOLLAR TO BE PAID.

Before the Lincoln Club of Cincinnati, June 23, 1883, the Judge said :

"You all remember how, under the name and banner of the Democratic party, especially here in Ohio, all the disloyalty, faithlessness and demagogy of this country seemed to clasp hands, and join in a common effort to besmirch and disgrace and dishonor that country and that government which the enemies of the government on the field of battle had failed to overthrow and destroy. You all remember how it was through long years of earnest argument and effort that the country was finally led back and placed on the firm rock of specie resumption, and the people were brought to a settled determination that all the obligations of the government should be faithfully paid to the last dollar.   *   *   *   *

PROGRESS FOR THE RIGHT.

But the mission of the Republican party is progress—and progress for the right; and where right and justice demand it, there is always a way to reconcile differences and conquer difficulties. We have never failed to find that way in the past; we shall never fail to find it now. Yea, we have already found it, and, as in the past, the defeats we have sustained have but served to the point, and give effect to the victories that have followed in succeeding years, so, too, will it prove that the defeat of last year will but serve to give emphasis and lend brilliancy to the magnificent triumphs of this. [Long and enthusiastic applause.]   *   *   *   *

GERMAN REPUBLICANS.

I say it is a slander upon the German Republicans of Ohio to say that they will withhold their support from the Republican party in this campaign. [Applause.] I think I know something of the German Republicans of Ohio. I went soldiering with some of them twenty years ago. [Tremendous applause.] With the old Ninth Ohio, made up of German Republicans living here in Cincinnati, I helped to carry our flag up the side of Mission Ridge. I was with them in such a way that I know what they endured of the privations and hardships of a soldier's life. I know how they bared their breasts to the storm of battle, and with what loyalty, devotion and patriotism they at all times stood by the flag, the country, and the cause of their adoption. [Ringing applause repeated several times.] Yes, I know, too, something about them since the war, and in time of peace. I know that the German Republicans of Ohio are an intelligent, fair-minded, liberal-minded, and honest-minded class of people, who have cast in their lot with us in good faith and for good purposes. I know that they believe in good government, in the protection of society, and in advancing the welfare and best interests of their commonwealth, as much as do any other class of people we have in the State of Ohio. [Great applause.] And being of that class of people, I say it is a slander, and a libel upon them, to say and print it of them, that they will withhold their support of the Republican party simply because it has enacted legislation that is manifestly just.

On August 2, 1883, before an audience of 2,000 people the Judge spoke at Corning, Perry Co., Ohio: *   *   *   *

PERRY'S VICTORY.

" There is something in the name of *Perry* County, for, when that name of Perry County is spoken it instinctively recalls one of the most illustrious heroes that this country has ever produced. ["Good!"] And along with the recollection of the old hero comes back fresh to our minds one of the most brilliant achievements of which the naval history of this country gives us any account.

THE COLORED REPUBLICANS.

And I want to say to these colored men whom I see so well represented here to-day that they do well to come up to this Convention along with the other Republicans of Perry County. [Applause.] Let me say to you, colored men that the next time you go up to the State House at Columbus —that place where I expect to hold for—for two years after the next election [laughter and applause]—you will be pleased if you will go into the rotunda and look at that magnificent oil painting which adorns its walls ; the title of it is "Perry's Victory on the Lakes." You will be pleased because you will see there in the boat, along with the old Commodore, in the thickest of the hail and storm of battle, and as brave looking as any of them, a fit representative of the African race. And thus it has ever been from the very formation of our Government — in war and in peace, in prosperity and in adversity alike—the colored man has stood side by side with his white brother. He has been with us in war; he is with us in peace. He has been with us to share our adversities ; he has been with us to participate in the triumphs that we have been permitted to enjoy.

LITTLE PHIL.

Another reason why it is a pleasure for me to be present here to-day is in the fact that within the boundary lines of Perry County is to be found the birth-place of another illustrious American citizen—a man who was as great a Captain on the land as Perry was on the sea—a man whose name is a familiar "household word" the world over—a man whom fifty thousand of us followed, with an admiration and confidence that no language can describe, as we carried that flag [pointing to the stars and stripes waving above him] up the rugged sides of Mission Ridge, sweeping Bragg and his regiments from off its crest, capturing more than sixty pieces of artillery and more than three thousand prisoners, and breaking forever th backbone of the rebellion. [Applause.] I need not say that I refer to gallant little Phil. Sheridan ! [Great applause. A voice : " Bully for the Irish !"]

A county which so reminds us of two such men as these is a county to be congratulated. Pataiotism is safe here.   *   *   *   *

THE TARIFF.

" How are you to tell in this month of August, 1883, how much tariff this country will need in 1884? How are you to foresee the expenses of Government? How are you to foresee a year ahead whether you will have an expensive Government or an inexpensive Government ? Whether you will be put to a great expense or a little expense in administering the affairs of this great Nation ? And if you can not foresee that, how can you tell how much duty to put on this, that or the other thing, to the end that you may raise just enough revenue to meet the wants of the Government economically administered ? And then another thing—are you to change this tariff every year ? It costs some years more than it does others to administer the affairs of Government. We have more pension bills to pay some years than others. We have more Indians to feed some years than others. We have more expenses of various kinds some years than others. If we are to regulate our tariff by the expenses necessary to be met, we must, necessarily, each year, vary the duties that are to be levied on our imports. And what kind of an effect will that have on the business of this country ? If a man must buy a product that is to be imported for him from another country, to be used in his business in this country, how can he tell what he is to pay for it when he does not know that the tariff may not be changed in the time intervening between his order and his receipt of his article? Therefore, I say it does not affect the objection I make to the duplicity of this platform for Judge Hoadly to turn and ask me whether I want a tariff levied that will be more than enough to sustain the Government when it is economically administered. It only shows its weakness.

Of his New Philadelphia speech, Aug. 5. 1883, the Journals said that "Although the Judge spoke in the open air, in the broiling hot sun, the audience of thousands remained attentive to the last word. The Judge never slacks speed or rises in the air, pays no attention to wayside 'funny business,' but makes straight for his goal." The Judge thus spoke:

THE NATIONAL GOVERNMENT SUPREME.

"What lawyers and the statesmen of the country could not settle satisfactorily—the constitutional question as to the character of our government, the North contending that the Constitution was the organic law of the whole land and people, and that our National Government was supreme over States and people alike—that question "the boys in blue" settled in the storm of battle. They wrote a decision upon it; they wrote it with the bayonet; they wrote it with blood; they wrote it where it would do the most good—they put it into the Constitution of the United States, and they put it there to stay. [Enthusiastic applause.]

And thus it was that the heresy of secession, the infamous product of the resolutions of 1798, and one of the most vicious of heritages to the people of this country, existing as a continual threat and menace to our institutions and prosperity—that idea of secession, I say, perished, and I trust passed away from American politics forever amid the burning glories of the triumphant victory at Appomattox. [Immense applause.]

FOUR MILLIONS ENFRANCHISED.

Well, as a consequence, in that great struggle which the Republican party came into existence for the purpose of carrying on, we had the shackles stricken off of four millions of people, and as a result of the reconstruction measures that followed, four millions of people and their colored brethren everywhere throughout the United States were lifted up to the plane of citizenship. They were enfranchised. Thus, for the first time, we had in this country "personal liberty" for every man and equality of rights for every citizen; so that every man who looked upon the folds of that flag (pointing to one floating before him from the staff in the public square) with the allegiance of citizenship, looked there knowing that it was symbolical of defense for him and of protection for all his rights.   *   *

CONVICT LABOR.

We don't believe in putting our laborers into unjust competition with foreign laborers, or into unjust competition with degraded home laborers; for we believe that the honest laborer outside the penitentiary—who has never committed any crime, and who has to support himself and family—should not be brought on a level as to his labor with men who have been confined in the penitentiary for the commission of offenses. For that reason, while we say these men should be made to work, we also say they should be made to work in such a way under the supervision of the State in some manner to be devised, as to prevent their work being brought into competition in an unjust manner with the labor outside.

www.ingramcontent.com/pod-product-compliance
Lightning Source LLC
Chambersburg PA
CBHW022152090426
42742CB00010B/1487